TEST MATCH SPECIAL

HOW TO READ
CRICKET

Also available from BBC Books

Tall Tales: The Good, the Bad and the Hilarious from the Commentary Box

The Test Match Special Book of Cricket Quotes

The Test Match Special Quiz Book

The Wit and Wisdom of Test Match Special

50 Not Out: The Official History of a National Sporting Treasure

TEST MATCH SPECIAL

HOW TO READ CRICKET

Everything you need to know about the greatest game in the world

By Ebony Rainford-Brent with Nick Constable

BBC BOOKS

UK | USA | Canada | Ireland | Australia
India | New Zealand | South Africa

BBC Books is part of the Penguin Random House group of companies
whose addresses can be found at global.penguinrandomhouse.com

Penguin Random House UK
One Embassy Gardens, 8 Viaduct Gardens, London SW11 7BW

penguin.co.uk
global.penguinrandomhouse.com

First published by BBC Books in 2025

1

Copyright © Ebony Rainford-Brent 2025
Illustrations © Matthew Burne
The moral right of the author has been asserted.

Penguin Random House values and supports copyright.
Copyright fuels creativity, encourages diverse voices, promotes freedom of
expression and supports a vibrant culture. Thank you for purchasing an
authorised edition of this book and for respecting intellectual property
laws by not reproducing, scanning or distributing any part of it by any
means without permission. You are supporting authors and enabling
Penguin Random House to continue to publish books for everyone.
No part of this book may be used or reproduced in any manner for the
purpose of training artificial intelligence technologies or systems. In accordance
with Article 4(3) of the DSM Directive 2019/790, Penguin Random House
expressly reserves this work from the text and data mining exception.

Typeset in 11.5/15.5pt Dante MT Pro by Jouve (UK), Milton Keynes
Printed and bound in Great Britain by Clays Ltd, Elcograf S.p.A.

The authorised representative in the EEA is Penguin Random House Ireland,
Morrison Chambers, 32 Nassau Street, Dublin D02 YH68

A CIP catalogue record for this book is available from the British Library

ISBN 9781785949500

Penguin Random House is committed to a sustainable future
for our business, our readers and our planet. This book is made
from Forest Stewardship Council® certified paper.

To the late Jenny Wostrack, whose unwavering support during the formative years of my cricket career was nothing short of inspirational. Jenny drove me across the country to trials, applied for scholarships on my behalf, taught me how to knock in my first bat and was there for me whenever I needed a guiding hand. Crucially, she made the game accessible and digestible, which is exactly what I've tried to do in this book. I hope I've channelled the energy Jenny brought into my life into helping others discover the game and grow to love it as much as I do.

Contents

Foreword	xi
My Story	1
One Game . . . But Which Format?	11
Actions	17
Batting	27
Coloured Balls	43
Data	49
Etiquette	59
Form	65
Ground	75
Howzat	81
Injury	87
Jinxes	91
Keepers	99
Leadership	103
Mind Games	113
Nervous Nineties	119
Out	125
Powerplay	145
Quick Singles	151
Rough	155

How to Read Cricket

Seam, Swing and Spin	161
Tours	175
Umpires	181
Village Cricket	189
Willow	193
X-Factor XIs	197
Yips	205
Zero	209
Glossary	215

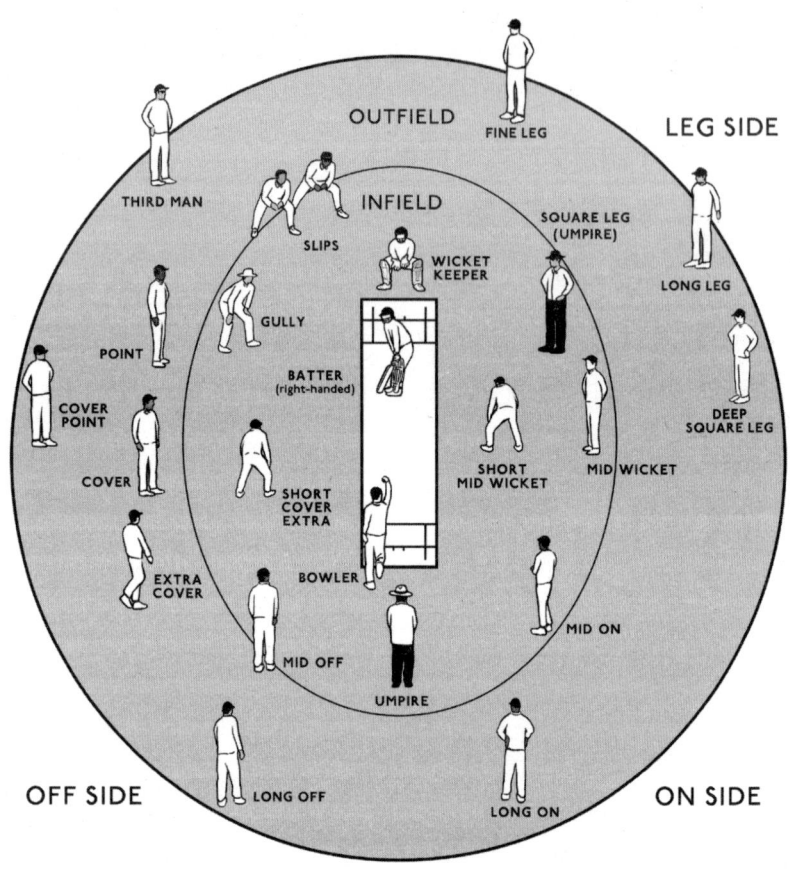

Foreword

I love the idea of demystifying cricket – spreading its unique joys among those who may perceive it as complex, even baffling. Its greatest attribute is that you can start playing in minutes, as anyone who has ever marked a crease in the sand for beach cricket knows. Get a ball, a lump of wood for a bat, a cardboard box for stumps and you're good to go. Bowl the ball, hit the ball, go for a run and, as Shakespeare's Henry V put it, 'the game's afoot'. The joy of cricket is that once you've got that basic understanding you can dive into the nuances of a sport that, uniquely in team competition, marries the head-to-head struggle between two individuals (batter and bowler) with the wider tactical tussle involving 22 players.

How to Read Cricket is not a book overly concerned with the practical mechanics of the game. It's not a coaching manual, although it mentions some of the basic skills required in batting, bowling and fielding. It's not an assessment of cricket strategies, although we'll consider how they change depending on which format of the game is being played. Neither is it a nerdy obsession with the Laws, although it's important to grasp some essentials because this is where the action starts and ends. Above all, this book is a peek into cricket's triumphs and failures, its customs and culture, controversies past and present, the brilliant and the bizarre and the extraordinary players who make it all so much fun. The game belongs to keen amateurs on village greens every bit as much as international stars plying their trade at world-renowned venues, and I've tried to capture a snapshot of my own journey from knockabout street cricket to World Cup glory. The A–Z format is designed so that readers can dip in and out of key themes and talking points, and I've included personal anecdotes that I hope will grab both the cricket obsessive as well as the curious rookie. It's the greatest game on Earth, and the next best thing to playing it is knowing how to read it. I hope this book will help you do exactly that.

Ebony Rainford-Brent

My Story

I never wanted to play a weird game like cricket. It was 1993, I was ten years old, growing up in Herne Hill, near Brixton in south London, in a single-parent household – my mum, Janet Rainford, three older brothers and me. There was absolutely no interest in cricket from any of us, even though Mum had a Jamaican background. Instead, we were obsessed with football. We all supported Liverpool, and I thought I was destined to be the new Robbie Fowler or John Barnes. Then one day this cricket coach turned up at my school, Jessop Primary. His name was Tony Moody and he worked for a charity called the London Community Cricket Association* set up following the 1981 Brixton Riots as a way of bringing the community – and particularly young people – together. In the early 1980s they were trying to entice more state-school kids into playing cricket and I recall my teacher taking me aside to ask if I wanted to give it a try. 'Well, no' was the simple answer to that. I'd seen cricket on TV. Everyone wore weird white clothes and they were forever stopping for lunch or tea or

---

* The LCCA is now called The Change Foundation and has expanded into other sports and the creative arts to provide opportunities for young people.

something. I just didn't get it. But the teacher kept on at me: 'You love football, you love sport, give it a go.' And so I did.

The moment is crystallised in my mind. We were in this caged playground at the school, and the coach was there. My teacher handed me a blue bat, they showed me an orange ball and said: 'Just hit it.' And I did. I walloped my first ball out of the playground into a park on the other side of the road, which happened to be quite near our house. Such a great feeling. You could hit the ball as hard as you wanted – that was apparently the whole idea. It may sound strange, but it was such a sense of freedom. I was hooked.

I signed up with Tony to attend his Saturday-morning sessions at Stockwell Park School, 50 boys and me. The gender imbalance didn't worry me at all because I had spent my entire life dealing with brothers and I had no problem holding my own. We played a version of street cricket called bowl-to-bat. It was quite competitive – you might even say aggressive – because you had to win the ball as a fielder to get a go at bowling. Then you had to bowl out whoever was batting to get the chance to bat. It was everyone for themselves and I'd be charging around, elbowing fielders out of the way, pushing them, slide-tackling them, anything to get my hands on the ball. I had so many holes in my trousers and poor Mum was forever patching them up. But it was great fun and the kids all got on well. We were a multicultural community, lots of first-generation born Brits, all from different backgrounds, and many of us have stayed friends to this day. I have life-long friendships forged through playing Saturday street cricket for three hours at a time.

Tony was a great coach. He made the game simple, relatable and fun. He got us transitioning from the soft ball we used in street cricket to a hard cricket ball by getting us to stuff the ball into an old sock and tie it up on a long piece of string attached to a tree branch or washing line. Then you grabbed a bat and practised your shots on it for hours. It was quite a common coaching strategy in those days because it was accessible for everyone. We were taught the hallowed technique of keeping a high elbow when executing a shot, and that's still a sound approach even though batting styles and techniques have evolved greatly with the rise of the limited-overs game.

Stockwell Park coaching was a couple of quid a session, which was a lot of money in our house, but Mum could see the excitement and joy in me, she was proud and her response was: 'if this means a lot to you, let's do it'. She couldn't have known what she was letting herself in for. Soon I was playing all over London and travel costs went through the roof. We'd be up half the night studying bus timetables and then have to get up for a 5am service that would connect with another bus that would get me somewhere near a ground somewhere in Surrey in time for a 9am start. It was exhausting before a ball had even been bowled. Mum accompanied me; she wouldn't have me travelling around on my own.

My first organised match was a Kwik Cricket* tournament at Arundel Castle in West Sussex, one of the most beautiful grounds in the world, and Tony took us there. Because every team was required to field two girls I was a hot property. The event was a culture shock for two reasons: firstly because it meant I was going to travel outside London, a big thing in itself, and secondly because I'd never seen such an incredible castle. There was this amazing slope, which we all immediately ran up and rolled down. We didn't win the competition

---

* Kwik Cricket is a fast and simple version of the game designed for children.

but we did quite well and I was spotted by a former Surrey Ladies player and coach called Jenny Wostrack who was way ahead of her time in trying to make the women's game more accessible. Her uncle was the brilliant West Indian all-rounder Frank Worrell so there was obviously something in the genes. Jenny contacted my mum, saying: 'Your daughter has got something. We need her to come and play for Surrey.' From that moment she was my mentor. I was about 11 years old and so lucky that she found me. Mum had three jobs – NHS receptionist, night shift at Sainsbury's, cleaning work here and there – and so she couldn't always get me to matches. She also had three other kids to bring up. Jenny stepped into the breach and made sure I could always play. She taught me things as basic as knocking-in a bat* – as well as filling in grant applications and generally fighting battles on my behalf. If you're going to succeed in any sport as a kid then you need people like Jenny and my mum to make it happen. I was playing for Junior Surrey aged 12 and that was the crossover point for me, the moment I decided I wanted to play cricket at the highest level.

I'd be lying if I said it was an easy decision because I loved all sport. During my teens I was selected for England Schools basketball and athletics squads (my events were the shot put and hurdles) and I played squash and football for London Schools. In football I was a striker – what's the point otherwise? – and lived out that dream of being a female Robbie Fowler. If there was any manner of sports club on offer at school, whether it met before class, at lunch or after class, I'd be there. Mum took the view that as long as I kept up my

---

* The process of knitting together fibres on the front of a bat's surface by hitting it with a wooden mallet. This hardens and protects it ahead of first use. Many bats are now knocked in at the manufacturing stage.

grades I could do whatever sport I wanted. Gradually, though, cricket became the dominant force in my life. Once I realised there was a chance of playing professionally it became my sole focus.

I started out playing for Surrey Women Seconds. I was quite a bit younger than most of them but it was a great way to meet the club captain and some of the big characters. Then I got my chance to step up to the first team. We were playing at New Malden and I was fielding at square leg. In my mind I was telling myself: *be keen, you've got to look sharp*, and I kept pushing closer and closer to the batter to the point that I ended up just a few yards from the stumps – more short square than square leg. The captain constantly tried to move me back, but I couldn't stop myself creeping forward. Then the batter belted a pull shot, straight at me. By then I was so close I had little time to react and as I dived for the catch I realised in a split second that I'd overshot. In another split second I calculated my options, which were either to let the ball go through my arms for four or halt it with a head-butt. I chose option two. I collapsed in excruciating pain, a giant egg came up on my forehead, my mum was on the outfield screaming and I got carted off to A&E. I'd been so desperate to impress, to be a ninja in the field, and I'd ended up a liability. But, as I later tried to point out, I *had* saved a boundary, albeit in unconventional style, and I *had* put my body on the line for my team. It didn't stop me being a laughing stock, though. I suffered banter about that 'head-butt' for weeks.

Soon after that I got a letter from the England and Wales Cricket Board, inviting me up to Trent Bridge to train with Junior England. It was addressed to Ebony-Jewel Rainford-Brent and I remember saying to my mum: 'I don't think they mean me.' Mum gave me one of her looks: 'Really,

Ebony? Because there aren't too many with that name.' In fact, I have three more given names – Cora-Lee, Camellia and Rosamond – and you can see why they left those off the letter. The reason I am over-monikered is that I was the youngest of four children and the only girl. Mum had always wanted at least one girl and had names lined up to honour various grandmas. But each time she got pregnant she produced a boy and so the names never got used. She saved them up, added more and by the time I finally arrived there was a bafflingly long list. Mum admitted that she even contemplated a few late additions and announced these to the registrar at the last minute, just as my birth was being recorded. Dionne was one; Randell another. The registrar gently pointed out that there wasn't enough room on the certificate and that four given names was probably enough for anyone, especially as two of them, like my surname, were double-barrelled. So Mum stuck with Ebony-Jewel Cora-Lee Camellia Rosamond. Years later this caused absolute chaos on scorecards and I even vied with Sri Lankans to get into the top-ten list of the longest names in cricket. I realised I would never make the grade on discovering that Chaminda Vaas's full name was Warnakulasuriya Patabendige Ushantha Joseph Chaminda Vaas.

My room-mate at that Trent Bridge training camp was Isa Guha, who would go on to become a brilliant England international player. She remains a close friend and a great colleague in media coverage of cricket. I was 14, she was 13, and straight away we got on like a house on fire. We'd sit in our room, chatting for hours, making tea, soaking up the excitement, and then be out training with the coaches and senior players like Lucy Pearson. At that time I was an aspiring fast bowler and Lucy was as quick as anyone in the English game. Just being alongside her, seeing her professionalism, her desire to improve, was a massive inspiration. A few years later she became only the second Englishwoman in 70 years to take 11 wickets in a Test against Australia, which says it all. For Isa and myself, it was a time when our careers were moving faster than I think either of us really expected.

I was initially seen as a quick, opening seam bowler who could smash a few runs in the middle, but once I'd broken properly into the Surrey senior team I started to open both the batting and the bowling. I liked charging in, trying to take batters' heads off, get them jumping around, targeting their toes – it was all part of the fun. There's no doubt that I sprayed the ball around a bit. But at that time there weren't as many women in the English game who were as quick as me and so I suppose I was forgiven. Surrey saw me as a genuine all-rounder, although that switched later on. Jenny Wostrack always told me I was a better batter than I was a bowler and she kept pushing me to work on my batting. She got me on to cricket scholarships and one-to-one coaching sessions and I'm so glad she did because when I was around 19 I suffered a nasty back injury that effectively stopped me bowling for three years.

Up until that injury, fast bowling had been my business. My debut for England came during a 2007 tour, a quad series in India. It involved the top four teams in the world – Australia, New Zealand, India and England – and I was brought along mainly to gain a bit of experience. Then our key fast bowler, Katherine Sciver-Brunt, went down injured and suddenly it was: *Ebony, over to you, you're opening the bowling*. We were in Chennai playing a strong New Zealand team in the baking heat on a slowish pitch. Not ideal for my debut. But once our captain Charlotte Edwards chucked me the ball, all I cared about was charging in and bowling as fast as I could. Lottie was among the best players in the world so simply knowing that she believed I could do the job was a massive confidence boost. There were a lot of no-balls, a few wides but I was bowling just upwards of 70 mph at that time, which was quick for the women's game. Not as quick, though, as Australia's Cathryn Fitzpatrick – then the fastest in the world – who seemed to get a lot more out of the pitch than anyone else. What a bowler she was.

Bowling in the heat of Chennai was one of the most punishing experiences of my early career. You'll sometimes hear players talking about a fast bowler being 'cooked' – in other words, the heat has got to her or she's bowled for too long without a rest. I would have bowled all day at Chennai if Charlotte had let me, but the truth is it wouldn't have done me or the team any good. You know you need a break when your arm starts to fall away, your follow-through isn't right and your rhythm – so important to a quick bowler – breaks up. You lose pace first, partly because you know that this will help retain your accuracy, at least for a while, but there comes a point when you're so tired that everything falls apart.

We didn't do too well in the quad tournament, although I did get my first England wicket – in the shape of Kiwi opener Suzie Bates – which felt very special. Unfortunately, the feeling didn't last too long because my back broke down later that year, spasming and cramping, and I effectively canned bowling. I told the England coaches it wasn't going to work for me, I had to stop and that instead I was going to be a batter. They were sympathetic but not slow to point out that I might not make it back into a team where my batting position had been No. 9. That sounded like a challenge, so it was off to Australia for the winter to make my case. I was playing alongside the likes of Karen Rolton – a superb Aussie batter and captain and my favourite player globally by miles. That winter got me scoring runs on good pitches, form I was able to take back home the following summer as an out-and-out opening batter. I was the leading run-scorer in county cricket that year, in no small part thanks to Surrey who were truly amazing in the way they supported me and helped me through a difficult time. I got back into the England squad at the start of 2009 – just in time for an ICC World Cup in Australia.

In the build-up games we were just unstoppable. Claire Taylor, Sarah Taylor, Charlotte Edwards, Katherine Sciver-Brunt – they were all on fire. I was an in-out-in-out squad player and my first game in the tournament was against Pakistan, opening the batting with Sarah Taylor, which for me was living the dream. Four years previously, when my back had gone, I'd written down that my goal was to play in the 2009 World Cup. Now here I was, playing as an opening bat alongside Sarah, in a team that had been battered in recent years but now feared no one. That 2009 run of winning the Women's World Cup, a World Twenty20 and a Women's Ashes series easily stands among the greatest years of English cricket – men's or women's – and I was so proud to have played a part in it. We fell off a cliff afterwards but fortunately everyone forgot about that. Three years later my playing days were over and I'd begun a new career in the media.

I feel so privileged that cricket has been my life from the moment I bashed that ball out of the school playground. It's taken me from the rigours of street cricket in south London, through years doing the rounds of youth and amateur club games, the step up to Surrey and county cricket, the astonishing realisation that coaches thought me good enough to play for England and the pure elation of being part of a World Cup-winning team. Since ending my playing career ten years ago,

How to Read Cricket

I've been able to see the game from a different perspective, both as Surrey's first director of women's cricket, managing championship-winning sides, and later as a broadcaster including regular stints with the BBC's brilliant TMS team. I've learned so much in the three decades I've been involved and yet barely a day goes by without discovering some new aspect of a sport that, for me, never stops giving. I hope to give you the essence of my experience in *How to Read Cricket*.

One Game . . . But Which Format?

I know, it's not an auspicious start for our aim of demystifying cricket. However, before we get into our A–Z topics, it's worth briefly clarifying cricket's main formats. While the Laws don't change unless the Marylebone Cricket Club says so (more on which below), formats and tournament rules certainly do. Games can be played as five-day Tests, 50-, 20- or 10-over matches and, with the birth of The Hundred in England, even 16.67-over matches (that's 100 balls per side, in case you were wondering). You'll sometimes see Tests referred to as the 'red ball' game and limited-overs formats as 'white ball' cricket (see C for Coloured Balls). On the international stage, the latter includes T20Is (Twenty20 Internationals) and 50-over ODIs (One Day Internationals). And, whatever the format, pink balls will occasionally make an appearance in day–night encounters under floodlights. But take heart: to the casual cricket-watcher none of this really matters. The point and essence of the sport remains the same; it's just that teams use different tactics to try and win.

Test matches

The clue is in the name. Because Test matches can last up to five days, they become protracted tests of a player's fitness, technique and mindset, a battle of wills between batter and bowler. Games can ebb and flow and gradually build into a compelling climax. Batters have longer to construct an innings while bowlers will probe away for hours to tease out weaknesses in the batters' techniques. Tests are nothing if not wars of attrition and, while to the novice spectator it can appear as though little is happening, in fact *everything* is happening. Each ball and run tells a story – a lower-order collapse, a sudden outburst of big hitting ahead of a declaration (see glossary) – and as time goes on so the tension mounts.

Tests can, of course, end in a draw, usually when evenly matched teams enjoy consistently favourable batting conditions, but a last-wicket stand to stave off defeat is among the most captivating of cricket scenarios. I once had to explain this to a baseball-loving American friend. 'So,' he said, in what I felt was unnecessarily precise language, 'they have three playing sessions separated by two eating sessions every day for five days. It always rains in England, so the playing goes on later. If it rains a lot, then it also starts earlier. And at the end of all this, you're telling me that maybe no one wins?' Well, yes. It's inevitable that the uninitiated are going to find Test matches perplexing. But to seasoned fans, this is cricket as high art.

The toss in a five-day Test is a major factor because the captain who calls correctly holds the reins of the day's play, at least initially (see L for Leadership). She can choose whether to bat or bowl and the received wisdom is to always bat first on a good wicket because the surface will deteriorate and make things a whole lot trickier later. The way the pitch changes over time – typically the result of footmarks, weather and soil structure – is what makes the red-ball game so captivating. At first, the playing surface may be a tame creature with consistent bounce; by day four it has become a dusty demon, peppered with treacherous cracks. Worn pitches are slightly less of a problem these days, because they're covered outside playing hours and few Tests last the full five days. Even so, a captain ignores the risk of deterioration at her peril. The adage is that if you win the toss you opt to bat. Alternatively, you think about it for a minute and then opt to bat. Yet bowling first can also be a good strategy – especially if a grassy pitch and humid conditions suggest pace bowlers will be moving the ball around (see S for Seam, Swing and Spin).

Limited-overs matches

My twelve-year career was played almost entirely in the limited-overs format. It included twenty-two 50-over ODIs and seven T20Is. Women's Test matches were rare in the 2000s – I was selected for only one squad – while The Hundred, a game of 100 balls per side, didn't even exist. Now all four of these formats are common in both the men's and women's games, while 10-over leagues are starting to emerge across the globe. Limited-overs cricket is a very different beast to its Test match cousin. If I'm batting in a T20 or a Hundred game, I can advance my team's victory chances exponentially by hitting a six. That alone will often 'win' an over because every ball is precious and scoring off each one matters greatly. Similarly, the bowler who restricts me to just two or three runs has won the over because she's put me behind my run-rate target. In a Test match, my towering six *may* turn out to be important but in the overall context of a five-day game it is likely to matter less. I will still have to face that bowler, and others, for much of the day as they seek to exploit some batting flaw – perhaps unleashing the odd bouncer or setting traps by tempting me into high-risk shots.

Risk v reward – all formats

The balance between risk and reward is always in a Test batter's mind when selecting shots. Wickets are valuable. Keep them in hand and runs will follow. In limited-over formats such as the Indian Premier League, Australia's Big Bash or England's The Hundred, this matters less. There's no point messing about; pretty much every shot you play *has* to be risky because the team that hits the most boundaries will almost always win. Permitting a bowler to sling down two non-scoring deliveries (known as dot balls) in a T20 over is therefore itself risky. Remember also that wickets are valued differently according to the format and state of the game. A team often pays dearly for losing top-order batters early in a Test because, with unlimited time, it makes sense to keep them at the crease for as long as possible. You want to bat for at least a day and a half and that means facing anything up to 200 overs. But if that same team has already accumulated 450 runs, losing the ninth wicket comes with barely any cost at all. In T20, and to an extent 50-over games, the scenario changes. It may not be ideal to lose batters in the first few overs but if it *does* happen it gives middle-order players more time than expected to smash runs from the balls that remain. And, in a tight T20 game, runs from the lower order can often be extremely valuable.

Custodians of the Laws

Cricket is thought to have started in south-east England around the time of the Norman Conquest. The earliest written record dates from the late 1500s but it wasn't until the mid-eighteenth century that the Laws began to be codified. This process was initially conducted at the Star and Garter dining club, a favourite watering hole of the gentry on London's Pall Mall. Some of its members went on to found the Marylebone Cricket Club in 1787, and since then the MCC has been internationally recognised as the custodian of the Laws, reviewing, redrafting and reinterpreting them at times as the game has evolved. Its role is sometimes confused with that of the International Cricket Council, the sport's governing body, perhaps because the ICC occasionally imposes specific playing conditions on the tournaments it oversees. But here's the thing: the Laws of Cricket are the same whether you're playing on the village green or in the 132,000-seat Narendra Modi Stadium in India. And that's somehow reassuring. No matter how many formats, coloured balls and playing regulations get thrown into the mix, cricket remains one big family.

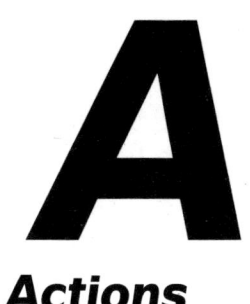

Actions

Your bowling action governs much of what you can do with a cricket ball. There are loads of variations but essentially there are two main types. Firstly, side-on, in which your chest is at right angles to the stumps and you're looking over your shoulder, behind your non-bowling arm at the target. That's the classic action for a bowler trying to swing the ball away from a right-handed batter. Secondly, there's chest-on, in which both chest and head are pointing straight down the pitch. This is typically favoured by bowlers swinging the ball into the right-hander. In either case the position of the feet is important. The aim is for feet, hips and shoulders to be aligned at the point of release. My problem as a teenager was that my action was mixed – some coaches would have described it as dangerous – because my feet faced one way and my shoulders the other. That forced me to twist my upper body in the delivery stride, which eventually created a serious back problem and threatened my whole cricket career (see I for Injury). The Surrey and England coaches spotted this and I had to spend an entire winter in the nets having my action remodelled. It was the most boring thing I've ever done. They were reprogramming muscle memory, and I had to walk through my new action, bowling tennis balls, for three to four months. Then I had to jog through it before finally getting the OK to run full pace. Even then it remained a work-in-progress. As soon as I was back playing, I would occasionally revert to my bad old ways, and it was another year before I could bowl the new action without thinking too hard about it.

There was also an impact on the *type* of ball I delivered. Before the remodelling, I used to get the ball to shape away from the batter; all of a sudden, because I'd switched to chest-on, I was moving it in towards the right-hander. That required a whole new game plan. I later discovered that my case was nothing new and that Test bowlers sometimes spend a winter fine-tuning their actions or ironing out small defects. They generally prefer not to do this, though, because it's not always clear what the consequences will be. Jimmy Anderson is a case in point: early in his Test career, when he was bowling at 90 mph, it was noted that he looked away from the target at the point of delivery. It was unconventional so his coaches tried to change it and, because Jimmy is the kind of pro always looking to improve, he took their advice. But in the end he ripped it all up because it demonstrably wasn't working. That can't have been the worst decision: among fast bowlers, he still became the leading Test wicket-taker of all time, with over 700 to his name. Provided a bowling action doesn't cause injury, Jimmy's experience suggests the proverbial wisdom holds good: if it ain't broke, don't fix it.

Chucker or bowler

Few insults levelled against a bowler carry as much weight as the 'chucker' jibe, the accusation that a ball has been thrown instead of bowled. Under Law 21.2 an umpire who believes such a transgression has occurred must call 'no ball' and may suspend a repeat offender from bowling again in the same innings. You might think the difference between a throw and a bowl would be obvious, but it sometimes takes hours of freeze-frame analysis to produce a definitive ruling. The wording of Law 21.2 isn't exactly user-friendly either:

> A ball is fairly delivered in respect of the arm if, once the bowler's arm has reached the level of the shoulder in the delivery swing, the elbow joint is not straightened partially or completely from that instant until the ball has left the hand. This definition shall not debar a bowler from flexing or rotating the wrist in the delivery swing.

ICC regulations state that bowlers with a naturally 'hyperextended' joint – in which the arm has a greater degree of flexibility – are deemed to be bowling fairly, even if to the naked eye they may sometimes *appear* to be throwing.

The most notorious chucking controversy concerned the greatest spinner in the history of the game, Sri Lanka's Muttiah Muralitharan (see below). More recently, allegations were wrongly levelled at India pace bowler Jasprit Bumrah following his side's first Test annihilation of Australia at Perth in November 2024. Bumrah took eight wickets for 72 runs and promptly received vitriolic abuse from some Aussie supporters (funny, that) on social media. Among those who defended him was the respected English bowling coach Ian Pont. 'You can see his arm straight from the wrist to elbow,' Pont posted on X. 'The rule is when it is above the vertical that the elbow must not bend past 15 degrees. You can clearly see the forward flexion in his arm, which is a hyperextension.

This is allowed (a forward bend) for people with hyper-mobile joints.' So now you know.

Muralitharan magic

This brings us to Muralitharan, who over a 19-year international career became the all-time leading Test match wicket-taker – 800 to Shane Warne's 708 – and picked up 534 ODI scalps along the way. Murali came on the scene at the time I was falling in love with cricket. I adored watching him, not least because he was always smiling, and he became one of my early cricketing heroes along with the entire Sri Lankan team. I was captivated by his action and shocked to hear people saying he was a cheat and a 'chucker'. The reality was that Muralitharan had a congenital abnormality resulting in his bowling arm being bent and hyper-extended at the point of release. This meant he was international cricket's first wrist-spinning off-spinner, which – and let's not get too nerdy here – allowed him to bamboozle batters with prodigious turn, a fast top-spinner and a notorious 'doosra', a ball that moved from leg to off with no discernible difference in action to his stock off-to-leg break. In 1996, after controversy at the 1995 Boxing Day Test in Melbourne when Australian umpire Darrell Hair 'no-balled' him seven times in three overs, the ICC referred Muralitharan to the University of Western Australia and the Hong Kong University of Science and Technology for biomechanical analysis. He was exonerated, and the ICC concluded his action merely produced the 'optical illusion' of a throw.

Gunning for Jenny

In the women's game there were similar rumblings about the England and Notts all-rounder Jenny Gunn. In 2012 she was reported to the ICC by two umpires, Phil Jones and Derek Walker, after taking two for 30 in an ODI against New Zealand. Clare Connor, then head of women's cricket at the ECB and chair of the ICC's Women's Committee, stood by her, insisting she would remain available for the rest of that New Zealand series. Neither was Connor impressed with the umpires' decision. 'Jenny Gunn's bowling action was independently analysed and confirmed as legal by the ICC in 2009,' she said. 'So, it is unfortunate for her that its legality has been called in to question once again'. In fairness to the umpires, having your action confirmed as legal doesn't make it *permanently* legal. It doesn't exempt you from getting no-balled for throwing. Watching Jenny, your first instinct was to ask yourself: is she chucking it? Her arm would go straight out and then appear to bend slightly in delivery. Yet the ICC tests proved it was perfectly legal. Digital technology allowed them to slow everything down, freeze-frame through her action and show that she was guilty only of having hyper-mobile joints.

The truth is that most professional bowlers in the pre-tech era of cricket had a dodgy delivery in their armoury, something one former England Men's player has described to me as a 'tactical chucker'. Instead of bending their back, they would be surreptitiously bending their elbow. It wouldn't be their usual action and they would unleash it only occasionally to add variation and pace – so much so that a spinner could produce a faster ball than an opening quick. Batters would often respond with carefully chosen banter – 'Have a look at that action, umps, that can't be right' – the aim being to ensure the tactical chuck was used only sparingly. My guess is that in club and village cricket, it is still alive and well.

Malinga the Slinga

Curious bowling actions are everywhere in cricket but few touch the extraordinary 'round-arm' technique of another former Sri Lankan icon, Lasith 'Slinga' Malinga. Malinga was a fearsome prospect. He would send down 90 mph deliveries with his right arm barely above shoulder height, producing fast in-swingers that homed in on a batter's toes like guided missiles. His era of international cricket was in the mid-2000s, at a time when Australia's Brett Lee was a contemporary. Lee was a 100 mph bowler, among the fastest in the world, but given the unenviable choice of facing one or other of them, plenty of Test batters would have opted for Lee over Malinga. When Brett was in the final stage of his run-up, he'd present the ball so that you could see its seam position and shiny side. Among current quicks in the men's game, Surrey and England's Gus Atkinson does the same thing. This provides a clue as to what the ball might do off the pitch (see S for Seam, Swing and Spin). There are other tell-tale signs: if the shoulder drops early then you're probably getting a short ball; if the body position at release stays upright then it'll likely be fuller. However, with Malinga, you got none of those signals. For one thing, his arm would disappear behind his back in the delivery stride so seam-spotting was out of the question. For another, the height of the arm and low trajectory of the ball made it difficult to tell whether you were getting an in-swinging fast yorker, a slow yorker or a wide ball outside off. His first-class career record of over 800 wickets speaks for itself, but what amazes me is that he was never dogged by persistent injury. Round-arm bowlers often do get shoulder problems, so maybe he benefited from an unusually mobile shoulder joint.

His finest hour came during the ICC 2007 World Cup in the West Indies during a group-stage game against South Africa in Providence. South Africa needed only four runs to win with five wickets in hand when Malinga cranked up the after-burners to spread panic in the Proteas' camp. First, he clean-bowled Shaun Pollock with a sublime slower ball, then unleashed a yorker at new batter Andrew Hall, who obligingly looped a catch to Upul Tharanga at cover. The first ball of his next over completed the hat-trick as Jacques Kallis nicked it behind to Kumar Sangakkara before Makhaya Ntini played all over another brutal yorker to be bowled for a golden duck. South Africa closed out the win but it was Sri Lanka who made it to the final, where not even the magic of Malinga could save them from a 53-run defeat at the hands of the Aussies. At the time of writing there has been only one other occasion in international cricket when a bowler has taken four wickets in four balls. That happened in Pallekele during the third T20I of New Zealand's 2019 tour of Sri Lanka. You can probably see what's coming – unlike four of the Kiwi's top five batters: Colin Munro, Hamish Rutherford, Colin de Grandhomme and Ross Taylor. Slower and older (now 36) but still the master, Lasith Malinga – for the second time – dismissed four in four balls. No wonder Sri Lankan youngsters still mimic his action today. Of the current crop, Matheesha Pathirana, who the media have dubbed 'Baby Slinga', has recently broken into the Lions' limited-overs sides.

The DRS dodgy debut

One last thought on Murali, who played alongside Malinga between 2004 and 2011. How many more wickets would he have taken if the Decision Review System (see H for Howzat) had been introduced at the start of his international career rather than 16 years later? That said, there is a smidgeon of irony about the way Murali bagged the first ever DRS wicket in a Test match because it should never have been given out. The controversy occurred during a DRS trial in 2008 – the first Test between Sri Lanka and India, in Colombo. Four Sri Lankan batsmen posted centuries, the hosts rattled up 600 for six and India were taken apart in both innings as Murali bagged 11 wickets for 110, ably assisted by his spin partner Ajantha Mendis (10 for 98). DRS wouldn't have made a blind bit of difference to the result, but third umpire Rudi Koertzen's use of it in the dismissal of India's opener Virender Sehwag had cricket's chattering classes in full cry. Bear with me here; things get a little convoluted but it's a good example of how, even with the benefit of technology, umpires can make mistakes.

On the fourth day, Sehwag padded-up to Murali's last ball before lunch, convinced it had landed *outside* leg stump and had therefore eliminated any risk of lbw. Murali disagreed and appealed, umpire Mark Benson ruled Sehwag not out and Sri Lankan captain Mahela Jayawardene referred that decision to third umpire Koertzen. On reviewing the TV footage, Koertzen reversed Benson's on-field decision, instead concluding that the ball had struck Sehwag's back pad in front of middle stump – a clear lbw. But Koertzen had missed a crucial factor: after pitching, the ball had *first* struck Sehwag's front pad – barely in line with leg stump – and only then was it deflected on to the rear pad. That should have meant there was too little evidence to give Sehwag out. By the time the error – human not technological – was discovered, it was all too late.

B

Batting

When I began playing cricket seriously, English batting coaches were strictly old-school devotees of what you might call the Lord's manual. You had to play with a high elbow, show the full face of the bat, get into position for the short ball by stepping back and across your wicket to execute a pull. Or, if playing a cut, step back and across – they loved that phrase – then turn and rotate your shoulder to hit square or behind point on the off side. The reality, of course, was that in the modern women's game you didn't have time for any of it. Balls would come on to you too quickly and, by the time you'd done all that stepping back and across and rotated shoulders, you would have been smacked straight in the chest. Having been convinced as a kid that a batter's job was to 'just hit it', lectures on technique and the correct way of doing things were anathema to me. My background was street cricket, lots of flair and wristy shots and, although I didn't grow up playing alongside Caribbean cricketers, people would describe my style of batting as distinctly Caribbean. I wouldn't say I was rebellious during my academy years – I had to keep the coaches happy – but once their eyes were off me I'd go back to my own game. At one England camp a coach even told me to 'put that flair away' because he wanted me to do the whole back-and-across thing while cutting short bowling in the nets. However, I would move forward to hit the ball in front of square, almost an uppish drive, and I'd say: 'What does it a matter? A four is a four is a four. What's the difference if I'm hitting that four consistently?' It marked me down as a bit confrontational on occasions.

Bowlers were also expected to conform. I do wonder whether actions like those of Lasith Malinga or Jasprit Bumrah would ever have made it through the pre-2000 era of English coaching because they weren't sufficiently 'side-on' at the point of release. Of course you need a manual, not least to prevent young players from developing dangerous bowling actions (see I for Injuries), but that doesn't mean a manual has to be so restrictive that it dulls a player's natural ability.

Protective gear

Because of my height, I had to buy protective leg pads designed for large boys or small men. It wasn't easy to find the right fit and even now women struggle to get pads that are both comfortable and practical. In my case, the straps were always way too long and the trailing ends would flick against each other in the middle as I ran along. I'd get told off by umpires because of this – they would complain that they couldn't tell whether I'd got a nick behind off the bat or whether it was just a noise from the flipping, flapping pads. The other big irritation for me involved putting on inner thigh pads. That was an hour of your life you'd never get back. We didn't have to use boxes, though. Oddly, I get asked an awful lot whether women have to wear them. Maybe a few do, but most female cricketers don't bother. If we're hit there, we just get on with it. It's a different kind of pain to that experienced by male players. There's an old joke that the first cricket box was worn in 1874, but the first cricket helmet didn't appear until 1974 when men realised their brain also mattered. I'm not sure about the historical accuracy of that claim, but there's no doubt that the one piece of gear that can save your life is a helmet and no one should face any serious fast bowling without one. I didn't like wearing them – not least because of the heat factor.

Heat has a massive impact on performance. Even with vents, the temperature inside a helmet builds up over time and on a hot day it starts to become enervating. I'm of West Indian heritage but I've lived in England all my life and I'm not used to long periods of extreme heat during matches. Before one Australian club game we were told there would be loads of drinks breaks because the temperature forecast was brutal. I was out in the field – I wasn't even wearing a helmet – and there came a point when I realised I couldn't see the ball coming at me. It felt like a dream world. My teammates were laughing, telling me to get on with it, but despite all the hydration I had heatstroke. It was forty degrees. I had to go off, and even the next day I felt completely dehydrated and disorientated.

A study by the cognitive science unit at the University of Northumbria conducted a trial in which colts from Durham County Cricket Club were asked to bat in the nets for a while. Half of them wore standard, non-vented helmets and once they had finished the session they were plonked in front of a computer to be tested on their reaction times, attentiveness and vigilance. The team leader, Dr Nick Neave, found that a hot head had no effect on their ability to complete simple mental challenges, nor on their physical responses. However, when set more complex tasks requiring quick decisions, reaction times dropped as much as 16 milliseconds. That's the difference between hitting and missing a 90 mph delivery in the 0.45 seconds it takes to travel from the bowler's hand to the batter. The test was done in a cool climate, so you wonder how much more conclusive it might be in the heat of an Australian summer. Nonetheless, Dr Neave was clear that players should always wear protective helmets against fast bowling.

Opening the batting

Opening is a special skill, a different mindset. In some ways it's the easiest of the top-order positions because the bowler often needs time to get into a rhythm and find the best line and length (see below) for the pitch conditions. While she's working this out, it's difficult for her to instantly dictate to you and restrict opportunities to make shots. But you do still have to be mindful of the conditions. I realised early on that I needed to get better at reading wickets. Is the surface green overall or is there at least the odd green patch in areas where the ball will pitch? If so, the ball's seam could bite as it bounces and change direction (known as 'seaming' in cricket jargon), giving me little time to react. Is it damp and therefore liable to be cut up by the bowler's studs as she follows through? That rough ground could help the spinners. Does it look dry and dusty, perhaps starting to break up in places, which could at the very least mean variable bounce? These considerations are as important for club and village cricketers as for the professionals. In fact, more so, as pitches in the amateur game will rarely match county or international standards. Depending on the game format, the opener's job varies enormously. Is she there principally to protect her wicket and accumulate runs carefully and steadily or to smash boundaries from the first ball? And can she change tactics adeptly as the game progresses? To an extent, these skills apply to all batters but they're particularly relevant to openers because they set the early pace of the innings. And whatever the strategy, an incoming batter will often exchange a few quick words with a dismissed opener along the lines of: 'What's the pitch doing?'

Taking guard

To the casual cricket observer, this must seem bizarre. Why the big fuss about where the batter stands in relation to the stumps? What's going on with all that scraping of studs and hammering of bats on the crease? It's important because where you stand affects your ability to play your shots, successfully decide which deliveries to leave and even muddle the bowler's calculations about where she pitches the ball and the line she bowls down. I had to learn so much about which guard to take to which bowler. That's partly because in my early years I was playing a lot against men and you bat differently to them. They bowl faster than women, meaning the angle of the shot may be different. For example, you might be comfortable pulling a ball from a female bowler in front of square, but against a male bowler a similar delivery comes on to you faster and you need to pull behind square. My one-to-one coach at Surrey was Jeremy Greaves, who still works there in the Academy. I'd go in two or three times a week for sessions with him and that's where I really learned the craft of batting. I was working alongside people like Rory Burns and Jason Roy, attending training camps in India – all this helped me get my head around the subtleties of the game.

Line and length

I sometimes get asked by young players to explain the term 'good-length'. A length is just a way to describe the point a ball bounces, relative to the batter. A batter has a basic decision to make: does she step forward to the incoming delivery or does she step back? If the ball is full – in other words, if it bounces closer to her – the logical response is to move forward and drive. If the ball is short then it makes more sense to step back and try to cut or pull. In the professional game a standard length is around 4–6 metres from the batter; if you can pitch the ball within that margin you're on the money. That's because it causes uncertainty in the mind of your opponent. It's awkward. It's not obvious whether the batter should be moving forward or back. It also affects the integrity of her shot because the ball tends to bounce at an angle that produces a point of impact higher up the face of the bat.

Line can be defined as the flight of the ball as it flies towards the stumps. Is it travelling directly towards them or is the 'line' to the left or right? In Test cricket you generally want a line a little outside off stump – the Australian fast bowler Glenn McGrath was the absolute master of this – because the batter then has to decide in tiny fractions of a second whether to play or leave the ball. That line also offers the best chance of getting a nick off the bat to your wicket-keeper or slip cordon. If you can stick to that line and bowl a good length, as McGrath invariably did, you will eventually frustrate all but the very best batters and force a mistake. In the limited-overs game, it's different. You're more likely to bowl directly at the stumps, restricting the batter's shot selection and giving yourself the chance of an lbw shout. You also want to avoid being too predictable because otherwise good players will line you up and make hay. Shane Warne's rule was never to bowl the same ball twice in the same over; he would mix it up, vary line and length, spin the ball both ways, slip in a slower ball or some top spin – anything to keep the batter second-guessing. Essentially a game of cat-and-mouse.

Specialist batters

Specialists have really come to the fore in T20 and one-day games and are increasingly important in the Test arena. Put simply, you can place them into three 'tactical boxes'. There's the Fast Starter, who looks to add runs quickly at the start of an innings, putting pressure on the bowlers. If she gets out taking risks, there's plenty of time for those coming in later to rebuild. Then there's the Middle Order Rotator. Her brief is to keep runs flowing steadily through the middle overs – rotating the strike to ensure the opposition doesn't settle into bowling at the same batter. Finally, there's your Death Overs Slogger. Her job is simple: smash fours and sixes. Of course, there are players good enough to take on any of these roles and, depending on the state of the game and the pitch, the roles may merge or change. But broadly, this is the game plan for most limited-over matches in what I'd call the new era for English cricket. That began after England Men's disastrous performance in the 2015 ICC World Cup (the third time in five World Cups that they'd exited at the group stage), prompting the captain, Eoin Morgan, to transform his team into a far more aggressive and dominant outfit.

No player sums up this new era – attacking from the first ball – better than Jason Roy, who for me is the ultimate Fast Starter. You can understand why the selectors went for Jason. I've known him from a young age – we came through the

Surrey Academy together – and you didn't have to watch him long to see that he was a completely fearless opening bat. He didn't have a complicated strategy; it was mainly about hitting strong shots straight down the ground. What made him special was his mindset, his determination to utterly dominate bowlers and rapidly take the game away from them. His view was that if, in the first six overs of a T20 or the first ten of a 50-over game, you get well ahead of your run-rate target while losing only one or two wickets, then you're probably going to win. He never worried about protecting his own wicket; his focus was to take down the opposition at all costs and throw them on the back foot. This has since become the model for opening bats in the modern game. They must play fearless cricket, especially during the Powerplay (see P), when there are only two fielders in the outfield. It's a strategy you increasingly see lower down the order too, even in Test matches, with batters such as Harry Brook rewriting the run-rate records. That 2015 shambles did English cricket a favour; no longer was the idea to just play nicely, play carefully and wait for the bad ball.

Rotators

The Middle Order Rotator tends to be a utility player who can adapt her approach according to the state of the game. Beth Morgan, of Middlesex and England, was a good example; whatever type of bowling was deployed, she'd have a clear game plan for picking up twos and singles. She was extremely fit, a fast runner and, crucially, possessed a plethora of shots, which allowed her to manoeuvre the ball into gaps in the field – nothing irritates a bowler more. I'd say the number-one goal of the Rotator is to look for the twos, to angle a shot between fielders, forcing them to chase the ball and allowing the batters time to get up and back. Often, a Beth Morgan-style Rotator isn't risking her wicket in the way she would be if she was belting boundaries, yet still she's milking the bowling, maybe even at 10 or 12 an over. She won't ignore the chance to sweetly dispatch the odd four or six but, because she's quietly racking up runs, there's less pressure to do so. She'll be comfortable playing the reverse and paddle sweep, the ramp, the hit down the ground – in fact, anything that makes the opposing captain move fielders around.

Good Rotators are among the smartest and most valuable of players. They can adjust to all conditions, knock any bowler off line and length, and help avoid middle-order collapses by managing risk. The best example of Beth doing exactly this came during the 2009 T20 World Cup semi-final against Australia. The Aussies had set England a target of 164 and, because I was on the bench in that game, I was able to properly analyse our response. The required run rate was over eight and, when Beth came in at 43 for two after seven overs, we were well behind. I suspect most of us would have tried to slog our way out of trouble, unsuccessfully, but Beth played a superb foil to Claire Taylor's magnificent knock – calmly rotating the strike, letting Claire play her shots, frustrating the bowlers and ultimately securing the win with an unbeaten partnership of 122 and three balls to spare. Plenty of players and commentators across both the men's and women's game now see her innings as the archetypal Rotator contribution, one of the greatest in T20 history. It was relentless – two, two, two – gradually chasing down the run rate, overtaking it, turning the pressure back onto Australia. It was wonderful to watch.

Death overs

In that game we didn't require a death-overs hitter. When the need does arise, you're looking for a player with brute strength who can clear the ropes even against the old ball, who is perhaps batting at No. 6 or 7 but can also hang around into the final overs. In the men's game the West Indies' Kieron Pollard would be an exemplar. In recent years teams have also worked hard on converting tail-enders into death-overs hitters, and England's Mark Wood is one product of that. He has an ODI top score of 43 and a Test half-century under his belt. He knows his job is to hit boundaries or, failing that, find what coaches call a 'release shot', passing the strike to a more accomplished batting partner. He's also blessed with what cricketers call 'a good eye'. Recent research shows that the best batters see the ball coming out of a bowler's hand earlier and watch it for longer. As you get older you notice that this ability starts to desert you, you don't pick up the ball so well and you fall back on experience and technique. Mark would never claim to be in the side for his batting and he hardly has a textbook technique – once admitting to me that he never works on it – but he sees the ball early and picks up vital runs down the order.

The slog specialist

In the women's game the greatest slogger I ever played against was the West Indian Cordel Jack. Suffice it to say, she was an imposing figure. When she first walked out to bat against us in the first T20 of the 2009–10 Caribbean tour, every fielder was having a quiet laugh, thinking: *This won't last long, no technique, no chance.* It proved a valuable lesson on the folly of judging a player by their appearance. Jack not only had technique, she had power to burn. During one over she opened her stance, flexed her forearms and hit us for consecutive sixes – the biggest I've ever seen in the women's game. It was one of those wow moments. She bashed a quickfire 39 and no one was laughing by the end of it.

Trendy lefties

Left-handed batters are among the most valuable assets in the game, especially when they're paired with a right-hander. That combination often unsettles the bowler's rhythm because she has to keep adjusting her line and length or to bowl from different sides of the stumps (round instead of over the wicket, and vice versa). Bowlers are so accustomed to bowling on off stump to right-handers that their muscle memory takes over and they keep the same line to a left-handed batter, which means an easy pull shot, effectively a free hit outside leg stump. Left-handers get used to bowlers making this mistake because most bowlers are right-handed. In the men's game Brian Lara was the master – he'd just sway inside the line and whack a boundary. Graham Thorpe and Mark Butcher were also gifted left-handers – you did not want to offer players like that a hint of width outside leg stump. In the women's game England had Lydia Greenway, of Kent, who was ruthless against wide deliveries. In the 2003 first Test against South Africa at Shenley, Herts, she was part of a record 203 fourth-wicket partnership with Claire Taylor, coming in at No. 5, rotating the strike, working the angles, frustrating the bowlers, and generally doing the job left-handers are born for.

The best bowlers have the ability to come around the wicket to left-handers and straighten up their line. I always struggled with that because my balance got messed up and my follow-through took me onto the protected area in front of the stumps. That's where studs can rough up the surface, giving an advantage to bowlers – especially spinners – at the other end. Umpires aren't slow to issue warnings if you do this, and you'll get only one more chance before you're suspended from bowling for the rest of the innings. I decided to stick to bowling over the wicket to left-handed batters. These were the days before Hawk-Eye and the Decision Review System and it meant I had less chance of getting a successful lbw decision – purely because of my angle of attack. It was a compromise but that's part of the game.

In the nets

Net practice is important for honing or correcting technique but it's not a silver bullet for improving form or confidence. I sometimes see batters having a long net session on the morning of a game and wonder whether they're scoring all their runs in there rather than out in the middle where it matters. The hard work needs to be done in advance. That means practising your range of shots, getting your timing right and sorting a game plan against bowlers you're likely to face. But there's no point in over-prepping on the day. A few throw-downs before the start of play, feeling bat on ball, that's all you need. I had to learn this. I was something of a nets badger, practising 24/7, working on shots before, after and even during games. In the end that became counter-productive and I realised that on match days I just needed to get my game head on.

Batters I loved as partners

Sarah Taylor was perhaps the most naturally gifted player I've seen, both with the gloves and the bat. She could work bowlers around the outfield at will. I remember watching from the other end as she scored a half-century against Australia at Chelmsford. We'd be chatting briefly in a break between overs, probably about what we'd watched on the telly, but then we'd see a new bowler coming on and I'd ask: 'Where will you hit this one, then?' She'd know precisely. It wasn't that she was determined to play the shot *whatever* ball she received; she'd just have a game plan for this specific bowler that told her most deliveries would be pitched outside off. 'Oh,' Sarah said, 'it'll be an in-to-out shot [the shape of the swing] over extra-cover.' And it was. First ball. Sarah had this amazing mindset that let her play stress-free. She'd have a laugh and a joke and chat about all manner of trivialities out in the middle, but once an over was underway she would switch on, dominate the attack and score for fun. It was an infectious freedom that helped me relax into my own innings. To watch a player like her from the other end – it was the best seat in the house.

Hogging the strike

Sometimes a batter gets all the action while her partner at the non-striker's end is left to admire the boundaries and occasionally run a single. It can just happen that way, but I've played second-fiddle to partners who were so irritatingly good that they always managed to push a single at the end of one over so that they could start on strike for the next. It's known as 'hogging the strike' and England's Claire Taylor was a master of the art. When I was about 18, I was picked to open the batting with Claire for Redoubtables, one of the country's best-known women's teams, in an invitation match at Cheam, Surrey. The England selector Patsy Lovell was watching and this was my chance to impress. Claire was the in-form England batter, I was the raw newbie and I'd walked out thinking: *Brilliant, I can't wait to bat with Tayls*. Barely an hour passed before the spectators were clapping her half-century. I, meanwhile, was on three. I hadn't properly clocked that at the end of each over she'd called for a single and hogged the strike. I didn't mind and neither did anyone else; it was a privilege to watch.

Hogging the strike can be a legitimate strategy. If there's a proven batter playing with a tail-ender then that pair will try to ensure their main asset gets as much of the bowling as possible. But in other circumstances it can be an agonising process. Suppose one batter is on the brink of her maiden century. She needs only four runs to complete it and there's no danger of losing the match. Problem is, her team needs only four runs to win. If she isn't on strike, and her partner nudges a single, the situation instantly changes. Now she *has* to hit a four to get that century – a pressure shot under any circumstances – because if she runs three the game will be over and she'll be stranded on 99. This was exactly the scenario facing Maia Bouchier and Nat Sciver-Brunt in June 2024 as England chased down a low New Zealand score in the second ODI. Bouchier had already survived a tight lbw decision on 92, and her heart must have been pounding (see N for Nervous Nineties). She scampered her way to 96, only to find herself off strike. At the other end Sciver-Brunt, an accomplished batter, then had to suppress all her attacking instincts by blocking four balls – including a juicy full toss – to ensure the score remained unchanged until Bouchier could face again at the start of the following over. Bouchier then nudged a couple of twos to bag her first international century. 'I'm glad she got her ton,' Nat told me later, 'but I'm never doing that again.'

Coloured Balls

Red

There's a big difference in characteristics between the red ball – the 'cherry' – used in Test matches and its white equivalent, used in 50- and 20-over matches. England's Jimmy Anderson can make a red ball talk, given the right conditions, but he'd struggle to get significant movement under any circumstances with its white equivalent. In red-ball cricket even the selection of the ball is important. You want the darkest red possible because this indicates a greater depth of lacquer, a retentive shine and therefore a ball that will move off the pitch and through the air for long periods. I used to enjoy shining one up and getting the red dye on my cricket whites. As a quick bowler, it felt like a message of intent directed at the batter.

I started my career using a red ball across all formats. You could work on it, keep the shine and, when the top lacquer finally came off, you would sometimes get reverse swing (see S for Seam, Swing and Spin), which is a batter's nightmare. A red ball stays harder for longer so bowlers feel there's value in it – they get more bounce and movement – while batters like it because it comes off the blade faster, potentially increasing their runs per shot. In short, you get a more dynamic game. The downside is that a new red ball can move *too* much, and you miss your target line and length.

White

The white ball was adopted for ODIs and T20Is with the arrival of coloured team strips in 2000. White was easier to see off the background of that clothing – which is good for the crowd and those watching TV – but it also changed the way teams approached games. This is because the lacquer on a Kookaburra ball – the only brand used in these formats – appeared to deteriorate faster than its red equivalent. Combined with its flatter seam, this meant that later in an innings it didn't offer as much conventional swing through the air, so giving batters an advantage. They could trust it to keep its line, and booming shots that would have been challenging with a swinging red cherry were far less risky against the white ball. Bowlers had to adapt their tactics, which is why we now see more unconventional bowling, such as slow-ball bouncers, off cutters, wide yorkers and slow yorkers.

In 2011 the ICC made an even more controversial decision by ruling that each bowling end should have its own dedicated white ball during an ICC 50-over or ODI game. The reasoning was that a white ball got dirty too quickly, making it harder for TV viewers to spot and so negating the whole point of introducing it. Yet this switched the balance of the bowler–batter contest significantly in favour of batters. A ball that never got older than 25 overs would still produce conventional swing, albeit not as much as its red counterpart, but it would never deteriorate enough to produce the rough surface required for a pace bowler's most feared weapon – reverse swing. Speaking during the Men's 2023 ICC World Cup, one of the great exponents of that technique, Mitchell Starc, insisted that 'one-day cricket should be one ball'. He went on: 'If you look at some of the old footage, when they bowled with one ball, reverse swing comes into it a lot more. That brings the bowlers back into the game, and I don't think it's any secret that one-day cricket and probably T20 cricket as well is a batter's game and bowlers just have to hang on.' Spinners are also unhappy with the two-ball rule. The Indian batting legend Gautam Gambhir, appointed India's head coach in 2024, has pointed out that finger spinners rely on a roughened ball to get grip and increased rotation. 'The worst thing that has happened in cricket is the introduction of two new balls,' he said. 'You've taken the entire skill of a finger spinner away from the game, whether it's a left-arm spinner or an off spinner. You've got two new balls, you've got five fielders inside [the circle – see P for Powerplay], how do you expect a finger spinner to get anything out of a surface and how do you expect a finger spinner to be included in the playing XI?'

Pink

I don't know any players who like the pink ball, now de rigueur for day–night matches. It was introduced because, once floodlights come on, a white ball starts to appear yellowish and harder to see. The problem is that during daylight hours a pink ball offers very little to the bowlers but after dark, as the dew comes in, it can start moving around like crazy. There's no settled explanation for this but many players

How to Read Cricket

feel it has something to do with different dyes and lacquers. Science no doubt holds the key but there are a lot of variables in how a ball behaves – the atmosphere, the pitch, the dew, the bowler – and there remains an air of mystery around the whole debate.

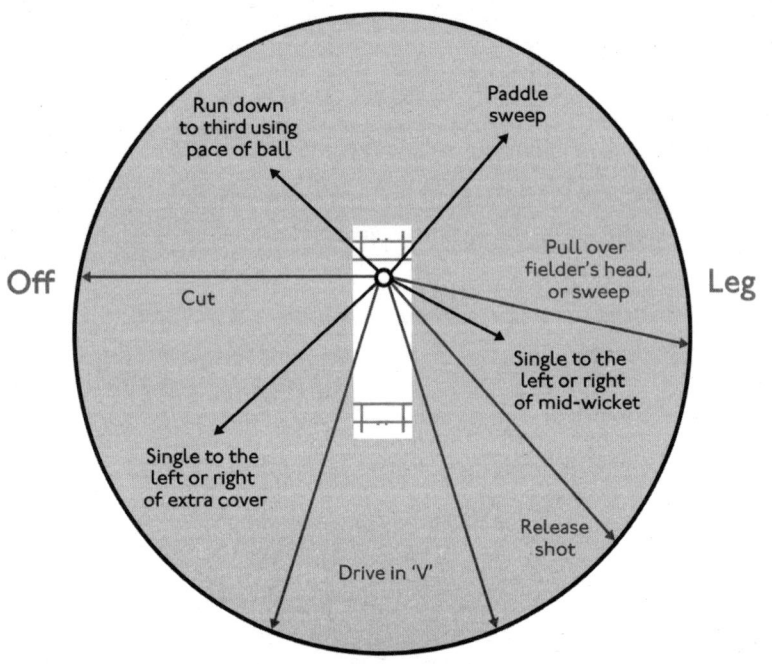

Data

The business of properly analysing your game – by which I mean analysing both your team's overall performance and your individual strengths and weaknesses – revolutionised Surrey's women's squad. There was a shift from playing matches with a few vague goals in mind to embracing the data, grasping what worked and nailing down targets. I was around 19 at the time and keen to impress our new captain, Mel Jones, a World Cup-winner with Australia, by buying in to this. But we started slowly. Mel asked everyone what they felt a decent score should be in a typical women's 50-over match. We studied the historical stats and concluded that if you posted 180–200 you won 89.5 per cent of the time. Mel said: 'OK, we're going to back ourselves to do this but if we fall short then we're going to stay behind and run the missing runs. It will be a collective reminder to think our way through games.'

This didn't sound too bad, but Mel was hard-core. I remember one tough match in which we fell 50 runs short. That meant we each had to sprint 50 singles, roughly a kilometre, straight afterwards when everyone was already knackered. Very quickly, players started chucking up. It looked like a mass outbreak of norovirus. God knows, it couldn't have been nice for the ground staff. We hated the way Mel had rocked up from Down Under to start punishing us and generally making our lives hell. However, she won us over because (a) she was obviously an outstanding cricketer and (b) she was up for a party once the hard work was over. She also got everyone thinking about stats and data and how it might help. We started to look at what we should be scoring in specific phases of a match – between overs one and five, five and ten and so on. Australia was far ahead of other cricket nations in terms of deploying analytics and, although we were coming from a low base, we'd at least made a start.

Today, full-time analysts are the norm. They'll tell you which shots you hit, how often you hit them, where you hit singles, where you hit boundaries and how much you score in each phase of a game. They'll identify match-ups, a useful in-play weapon for batters because these reveal the bowlers they've done well against and the ones who have troubled them. I was strong against off-spin but found leg spinners tricky, so if I was batting with a partner who could handle leggies we'd look for singles to manoeuvre her into facing her best match-up. These analytics have become a key part of the game and you can sometimes spot their influence – a wicket falls in a limited-overs game and the successful bowler is immediately taken off by her skipper for no obvious reason. Years ago, that bowler would get pretty miffed. You'd see her stomping off, head shaking, perhaps directing a potty-mouthed diatribe about her captain's parentage towards anyone in earshot. These days, it rarely happens; a bowler may not like it, but she will understand that she's been taken off because an analyst has crunched the numbers and advised that a team-mate is the correct bowling match-up to the incoming batter. Players can also check databases of videos. If I'm playing India, I can ask my analyst to provide recent footage of Indian left-arm spinners playing on similar pitches in similar conditions. That should tell me their stock ball, their usual variations and their most dangerous wicket-taking delivery.

Beware the data mantra

Data is one of the most important parts of the modern game, and AI software plays an increasing role in identifying match-ups, fielding positions and the best catchers. There are also virtual-reality headsets that let you see digital constructs of your chosen bowler running up and delivering a virtual ball, which you then play using a bat packed with electronic sensors. A readout gives you an instant verdict on whether your shot was any good. Another version of this is sometimes used in the nets. You'll watch, say, Jimmy Anderson approaching you on a giant screen, he bowls, the software analyses the track of the ball, communicates it to a physical bowling machine and down comes Jimmy's ball on the correct line and length for you to hit – or not.

Not all players like tech-heavy innovations and these shouldn't be seen as a silver bullet. Cricket is a game that still combines skill, fitness, luck and instinct. The data is not written in stone – in fact, sometimes it can undermine you. You head out knowing that you must hit this bowler into this space with this shot and then none of it happens because the bowler is following a different game plan. Similarly, as a fast bowler, you've seen stats showing that a particular batter doesn't like a ball shaping in to her body, but when you produce a few of those balls she works each one effortlessly to leg. What do you do then? You can't just keep following the data mantra. You have to adapt.

The best analysts keep their advice to one or two key aspects. They don't try to play the game for you. Some of the most useful briefings you get are nothing to do with you and your opponents as individuals; rather they provide your team with real-time information on what you should consider a good score, at this ground, in these weather conditions on similarly prepared pitches. It's pointless batting first with the mindset to score 300 when historical stats suggest 225 should be enough. Why play risky, high-scoring shots when you don't need to?

The true impact of data and video analysis in cricket didn't fully strike me until I retired from playing and became director of women's cricket at Surrey. That meant overseeing the Surrey Stars in the T20 Kia Super League and a season with the Oval Invincibles in The Hundred. I remember one player – I won't name her – who had a questionable relationship with the technology. If she was out cheaply or to a poor shot, she would stomp off and make straight for the monitor in the dugout to review what she'd done seconds earlier. Why do that? Why risk the upset and negativity of your bad day leaching into the heads of the players sitting close by? They can do without you rewatching your dismissal over and over or hearing your running commentary. You're sitting there, with your pads on, hearing someone effing and blinding about their shot when you're just trying to focus on your upcoming innings. The goal of data and video analysis is to look at these things in the cold light of day, making calm assessments on shot selection and technique away from the cauldron of tension that encompasses a game in play. Otherwise, you risk becoming obsessive. As a player you should never start going down the data rabbit hole in a search for answers because you can find almost any answer you want, depending on your interpretation. Good analysts know this. Their job is to add to your game, not take it over by creating experimental strategies that may not work and could even drain confidence further. The key is to maintain fluidity and adaptability, to be informed by analysis but not ruled by it.

Analysts work you out

A common fault in players is to stick with whatever's working. For batters, that means the shots they're comfortable with; in my case, it meant cut, pull or drive down the ground. Coaches would occasionally suggest developing a wider range of shots but that was something I didn't want to hear. Then one of them produced my wagon wheel – the circular diagram showing the direction of all my scoring shots – and pointed out areas I rarely found. There seemed to be quite a few. And if he could spot this then so could opposing teams, for whom I was effectively setting a field. Why bother with extra-cover or mid-wicket if Ebony never hits to those positions? I had to learn new shots, refine angles, give myself a bigger box of tricks. A good example in the modern game is India's Shafali Verma who in 2019, aged 15, became the youngest cricketer to play in a T20I. For around a year, she smashed bowlers into oblivion but then the analysts had a deep dive into her game and noticed comparatively few pulls and hooks in her wagon wheel. That's because she'd played all her cricket in India on slow pitches unhelpful to bouncers. Word spread round the circuit, as it always does, and once quick bowlers got her on a fast pitch, Shafali faced a barrage of bouncers. Her scores suffered and she had to be taught the technique to respond.

It must have worked because by October 2022 she'd become the youngest cricketer to score 1,000 runs in T20Is.

A wagon wheel is a simple, effective – some might say brutal – form of analysis because it highlights indisputably the weaknesses in your game. But it also tells a coach your strengths. Pull up, say, Claire Taylor's wheel and you'll see spokes stretching out every which way. A player like that becomes almost self-selecting. Setting fields to her would have been a nightmare. Whenever coaches see their side facing an emerging international cricketer, they will always look at that player's wagon wheel. This is particularly true in Tests, where there's so much more time to wear a batter down and expose potential weaknesses. If any weak spots are found, you can bet bowlers will target these ruthlessly while fielders will play mind games, telling incoming batters how their flaky hook shot, for instance, will soon allow them to return to the pavilion. Another data-fuelled trick is to remind an incoming batter how often they've been out to their match-up, say, your team's demon fast bowler. You shout over to that bowler: 'Here comes your bunny,' ensuring the new batter hears in the hope of playing on her nerves. And sure enough, next over, the skipper brings said bowler on.

Finding player value

As Surrey's director of women's cricket, it was my job to work alongside top coaches like Richard Bedbrook and Jonathan Batty to sign the right players. In theory we could go for anyone in the world – the 'stardust', in managerial jargon – but we had a budget to stick to and the need to liaise with international boards to get players released. We made the decision to target South Africans because, although many were on the radar of county clubs, they weren't getting picked up at the early stage of the Kia Super League because they weren't as well known as say the Australians. We felt they were undervalued internationally. The stats showed that when they were pitched head-to-head against so-called glamour players, they comfortably held their own and, in some cases, had 'bargain buy' stamped all over them. (I should emphasise here that 'box-office' cricketers are in no way a waste of money. They may cost more but they're a safer bet and their drive and commitment rubs off on the whole team.)

Lizelle Lee was a case in point. She wasn't perceived as another Meg Lanning, the Aussie everyone wanted, but I argued that if you looked at Lizelle's batting power, her destructive instincts and her strike rate – the number of runs scored per 100 balls – she was a comparable asset and was over-delivering against her key match-ups. We had two of her fellow South Africans locked in (one of whom, Marizanne Kapp, could single-handedly change a game with ball and bat), and we felt Lizelle had a complementary attack-minded attitude. Problem was, Lizelle wasn't sure she even wanted to play in England that summer. She needed convincing that Surrey Stars was right for her. This is where my playing experience helped. Signing players is not just about pitching a contract at your target; you need her mates on side and that can mean persuading *them* to help persuade *her*. Alec Stewart, who was director of men's cricket at the time, gave me great advice on this: in essence, hit the phone and start smooth-talking. We got Kappie in to help convince her and, bobs your uncle, we signed her.

Lizelle started with two ducks and averaged 6.25 in the first five games. The team only had one win on the board. I asked myself if her stats data was flawed and whether I'd relied too much on gut instinct. People I respected were hinting that they weren't sure about her. Had I got this badly wrong? She had a slight technical flaw affecting her leg-side game, and she and the coaches spent a lot of time addressing that – moving her guard to middle-and-leg and repeatedly running through a range of leg-side shots. But the main reason she was struggling was that her confidence was fragile after a tough start. On the eve of the 2018 Kia Super League final I told her that we backed her and valued her talent. I knew her motivation was to be perceived on the world stage as being up there with Aussie stars like Lanning and Ashleigh Gardner. We'd brought her to Surrey for a reason – that she was highly valued as a class performer. I finished with: 'This is your platform. The cameras will be on you. Go out and shine.' And shine she did. She smashed 104 in 58 balls, including six sixes, to take us to a match-winning 183 for six – the highest score of the competition. It was a huge high in her career. For me, it rammed home the importance of stats in uncovering overlooked talent across all areas of the game. All coaches want an attacking spinner who offers control, and they can now quickly compare who is bowling stump-to-stump, who regularly hits line and length and who puts most revs on the ball. We kept a South African feel to our side after that Super League win and our Ovals Invincibles went on to win The Hundred twice, in 2021 and 2022.

E

Etiquette

I've never quite bought in to cricket etiquette, those unwritten and often baffling laws that supposedly govern the spirit of the game. I generally followed them (with one notable exception – see U for Umpires) because we all had to. As a kid you get worn down and accept the status quo. Later in my career I decided some were just ridiculous. Like being a batter who 'walks', who gives herself out even though nobody has appealed, because she knows she got the faintest of snicks behind to the keeper. And there's a reason I changed my mind. As a teenager I'd always 'walked' if I knew I was out. That's because one of my elders in the club environment was the lovely Patsy Lovell, Surrey's most capped woman cricketer and later an England selector. Patsy would ram into us the principle that walking was the right thing to do because if you didn't you were a cheat. So that carried on until I began playing regularly for Surrey seniors at a time when our leading players included the Australians Mel Jones and Olivia Magno. If there had been a degree in cricket skulduggery then those guys would have taught it. They never cheated but they would do whatever was needed to give their team an edge.

On one occasion we were playing at the end of Surrey's

season and needed a win to stay in the top division. I was on 48, the last recognised batter at the crease, and we still required 25 runs. At that point I gloved the ball to the wicket-keeper who, together with the entire slip cordon, went up for a massive appeal. The umpire stared unblinkingly back and didn't move a finger. So I thought, *Well, I'm supposed to walk*. So off I went. The opposition and most of my team-mates were clapping and saying 'well done for walking', in stark contrast to Mel's first words to me: 'What the f*** have you just done?' The conversation continued:

> Me: 'I walked, Mel. I'm basically an honest person.'
> Mel: 'Ebony, that's the dumbest thing I've ever seen on a cricket field. You've just thrown away the game. Well done, mate.'

Here was the difference between club players, who were usually generous souls in a comparatively relaxed environment, and international players who had a do-or-die attitude to pressure. When the pressure cranks up, the etiquette crumbles. People may lament its loss and complain that the modern game has undermined the spirit of grassroots cricket, yet the argument against walking has gone on for decades at every level. In his memoir *White Cap and Bails* the late Dickie Bird, one of the game's best-loved umpires, recounted a conversation he once had with South Africa all-rounder Eddie Barlow. 'I've got away with a lot, Dickie,' said Barlow. 'I've been given not out when I should have been out. But, then again, I've been given out when I knew I wasn't. It's swings and roundabouts. Either way, I never complain. I go back to the dressing room, take off my pads and gloves and say nothing. I accept decisions, good or bad, because they even themselves out in the long run. But I *never* walk.'

Etiquette

Today, with all the technology available in international cricket, walking is no longer an issue. Hawk-Eye and the Snickometer (see H for Howzat) have seen to that. In a way, this has taken some of the drama out of the game because a 'non-walker' will always get players revved up. After that public dressing-down from Mel Jones, my decision to never again walk was put to the test in a match between Surrey and Sussex, with my England team-mate Sarah Taylor keeping wicket. I snicked a catch behind, the umpire hadn't a clue and so I stood my ground amid a volley of fruity comments from the slip cordon. A few balls later I snicked another and, as Sarah and the slips celebrated what they saw as my just deserts, I realised the umpire once again hadn't moved. So neither did I. He was having an absolute shocker and I stood there laughing my head off as the slips went potty. I'm a resilient character and I enjoyed the drama post-game as they lined up to tell me I was a no-good cheat and that I should be ashamed. Well, I wasn't, so pipe down.

In my defence, there have been plenty of times in club cricket that a fielder has claimed a low catch off my batting when it was blindingly obvious, to me at least, that the ball touched the ground before it was pouched. Sometimes, fielders will honestly believe a diving catch is valid because the ball has come to them fast at an awkward height and they've gone for it in hope without seeing it hit the grass first. Fair enough. All I'd say is that everyone wants to win, don't they?

Dress code

I have a few other etiquette bugbears. I don't understand the tradition of 'clapping in' an opposition batter as she walks to the wicket. Why do that? I know it's considered part of the game and is a nice thing to do but I was never too worried about being nice. I'd much rather win. Fine, give her a clap if she hits a half-century or century, but she's getting all this applause and she hasn't even played a shot. We're not here to encourage her. I loved it when my team-mates clapped me out to start my innings but that was a gesture of support, showing togetherness as a team. It was also the worst feeling in the world to slope off with a rubbish score and the ominous silence that tells you you've let everyone down.

The thing about respecting traditions in cricket is that they need to make sense, they need to be reasonable and there needs to be buy-in from players and supporters. At Lord's, home of Middlesex, the Pavilion famously has a formal dress code requiring men to wear a tailored jacket or blazer with a tie or cravat – who knew men still wore cravats? – and women to show up in a smart dress, skirt or tailored trousers with a top or blouse. Footwear must be 'appropriate to a formal setting'. This is all fair enough and I get that people enjoy dressing up for the occasion, but I still find it weird when I'm wearing a nice suit and a steward starts questioning me on whether my trousers are tailored. Perhaps it's because I'm a south London girl who wears high-top trainers whenever she can. Even so, it's an odd conversation to be having at a cricket match.

Pain of protocol

My favourite account of Lord's protocols comes courtesy of my TMS colleague and former England spinner, Phil Tufnell. In the mid-1980s, Tuffers was a rebellious teenager leading what you might call an overactive social life. For meals he relied heavily on the legendary culinary skills and maternal

Etiquette

instincts of the Lord's cook, a feisty Irishwoman called Nancy Doyle who had taken him under her wing. Phil would consume vast quantities of whatever was on offer – he once put away 15 of Nancy's lamb chops in a single lunch break. One morning, Nancy arrived at Lord's to find him asleep in his car. Tuffers rapidly perked up at the suggestion of breakfast and was instructed to head for the dining room – a privilege reserved only for senior players – where he was soon tucking into a fry-up alongside captain Mike Gatting and John Emburey. At this point two of the more pompous Middlesex committee men wandered over to speak to Gatt, one of whom loudly observed that 'second XI players aren't usually allowed in the dining room'. Unfortunately for him, Nancy was passing. 'F*** off, both of youse,' she said, equally loudly. 'Can you not see the boy needs food?' The blazer-types shuffled off, heads down, as Tuffers gleefully tackled another rasher of bacon.

It surely helped that he was sitting with his captain, who clearly had no problem with his presence. As a newbie, the one thing you never want to do is get on the wrong side of your team-mates. So don't stroll into the changing room on your first day and dump your coffin (a kit chest on wheels) any old place. It might be the favoured spot of a senior pro. If you appear arrogant before quietly sounding out who sits where, you'll soon be taken down. Established players will pick the prime seats where there's plenty of space, ideally an arm's length from the food and drinks table. Your goal is to hang back, hide away in a corner, wait until everyone's settled down, work your way into the pecking order and fit in wherever you can.

Form

It's an easy label to stick on a player – she's either in form, out of form or that catch-all phrase 'struggling for consistent form'. Stats don't lie in cricket, but rarely do they tell the full story. In truth, there are myriad reasons why form comes and goes, and these are not always obvious either to the player or her coach. You often don't know what's wrong and that's hard for a professional sportswoman to process. Is it a technical flaw? A lapse in concentration? A mental block? Stress and pressure? Poor shot selection? That niggling injury that you were so sure you could 'play through'? A subconscious bias in your game plan? Frustration that you're not getting selected?

It's a daunting list of 'maybes' and I was lucky to have Jeremy Greaves, my coach throughout my Surrey career, as a mentor who would invariably help me work through the possibilities, identify root causes and deal with them. For technical problems, one of his favourite methods was to slow everything down. My cover drive was usually fine, but there was a time when I started playing it too early and my bat would be halfway through the shot before the ball even arrived. Jeremy would get me in the nets with a few tennis balls and dolly these towards me, telling me to wait, wait,

wait for the ball, checking my feet position, my bat position, the lot. And, as if by magic, the correct shot came back.

As players we would also analyse each other's games. Within the England camp I'd do one-to-one work with Caroline Atkins. Even though we were both opening batters, both vying for the same position, we were also best mates and wanted to help each other improve. I was strong on dispatching short balls and cutting, which Caroline found more challenging, whereas I was a poor sweeper of the ball – something she did for fun. We'd go off to the nets on our own, play these shots and exchange advice.

Pressure moments

The ability to handle pressure at key moments in a game will often define a player's career, let alone form. Players can have decent mental strength, train hard and prepare well, but when the key moment comes – when the team desperately needs you to take a wicket, hold a catch or hit a four – not everyone steps up. Dealing with pressure is a skill that can be taught, and I certainly had to learn to stay calm using trigger words or phrases such as 'watch the ball'. (Incidentally, watching the ball is a skill in itself. Cricketers at grassroots level may convince themselves that they watch every ball right onto the bat, but in a run chase you'll see too many ugly swipes for that to be true.) Pressure is a strange bedfellow. The very best players seem to thrive on it, stay calm and execute the shot or ball required. For some of them, it's because they've had interesting lives, they've seen pressure up close and personal in work or family environments. There's a great story about Keith Miller, arguably Australia's greatest all-rounder, who played 55 Tests between 1946 and 1956. His image was of a

Form

devil-may-care playboy who as captain once famously told his fielders to 'just scatter' when they enquired which position they should take up. In fact Miller, a former wartime Mosquito fighter pilot, was a meticulous tactician who prepared game plans in minute detail and was scathing of any notion that players might be affected by pressure. He once told an interviewer: 'I'll tell you what pressure is. Pressure is a Messerschmitt up your arse. Playing cricket is not pressure.'

In the context he described, he's obviously right. But in professional sport mental blocks and stress are real and can be among the most difficult hurdles to overcome because there are so many potential causes. Sometimes, going for a drink with a trusted team-mate is enough to get you through it, although identifying the right person seems to become harder as you step up the levels; you don't want to let others know you're struggling in case word gets out and you get dropped. I would sometimes go outside the changing room to talk through performance problems, and on one occasion Michael Carberry, a classy England batter who scored hundreds regularly, helped me overcome a situation where I kept getting out in the eighties or nineties. I just couldn't reset, but Michael took me in the nets and made me play the same identical shot for three hours. It wasn't to fix my technique but about lengthening the time I could concentrate. And it worked.

Trying to correct any serious problem on your own rarely succeeds because you will almost certainly have a subconscious bias affecting your self-diagnosis. There's also a psychological demon, confirmation bias, that lurks in most of us. This is where you attribute cause and effect based on little evidence. Let's say you decide you're out of form because you haven't practised cut shots enough. So for a month you turn into a nets bunny and post a couple of decent scores. Problem solved. But then another poor run of form creeps up. Maybe all that practice helped but it didn't address the underlying flaw, which is nothing specifically to do with a cut shot. When you finally turn to a coach for help, you discover it's all about your shoddy positional footwork.

Fighting for your place

The vagaries of form create a strange dynamic because if you've not been selected for a game, there's a part of you wondering whether the team-mate keeping you out is going to have a bad day. It's not that you *want* that to happen; you don't *want* a mate to fail. It's just that if she does then it's your chance to shine. I faced this conundrum in August 2008 as England prepared to play an ODI against South Africa at Lord's. I was out of the side but had been waiting in the wings for weeks, desperate to regain my place as an opening bat. Caroline Atkins, who as I mentioned above was my best mate, and Sarah Taylor were doing the job and there was no way Sarah was getting dropped. But Caroline was struggling for form. Before the game the coach called me over and promised that if Caroline had another shocker, I'd be back in the side. Fantastic news. Except that Caroline and Sarah then put together an opening partnership of 268 – at the time, the highest for any wicket in the history of women's ODIs. Caroline got 145 of those and I felt every agonising one of them. I gave her a laser stare as she came off, thinking: *You little so-and-so, where did you pull that from?* She was mentally shot, her run-scoring was scratchy – surely she was destined to fail. Instead, she rewrote the record books. I had seriously mixed emotions. Happy for her, yes, but also fuming that she'd chosen this game, of all games, to show what a great player she was. Had the roles been reversed, Caroline would have felt the same. It's part of the game.

Lucky breaks

In an ideal world, your career as an international cricketer should be about objective skills such as technique, bowling armoury, shot quality, fitness and concentration. But there's another element that matters every bit as much: getting lucky. Or, at least, not unlucky. Cricket's history is awash with classy players who were given a chance at the top level but never established themselves. The potential reasons are legion. Perhaps a batter's debut required performing against some of the game's true greats – hands up if you'd have fancied starting your Test career in 1979–80 against that West Indies fearsome fast-bowling quartet of Andy Roberts, Michael Holding, Joel Garner and Colin Croft. Or walking out to face Shane Warne or Muttiah Muralitharan in their pomp. As for debutant bowlers, seeing names like Brian Lara or Sachin Tendulkar on the team sheet would suggest a long day ahead. There is therefore an element of luck to *when* you get your call-up. Occasionally, the 'never-quite-made-it' player is the unfortunate victim of an opponent's moment of brilliance – a curse that particularly affects batters as they don't have the bowler's luxury of ending one bad spell in the hope of finding redemption in the next. Batters suspect no one will remember *how* they got out, only that they did. By the time of their next innings, the pressure has marginally increased and their confidence has marginally dipped, and at international level small margins make or break you.

In recent years, Hampshire and England's James Vince

is a case in point. Vince made his ODI and T20I debuts for England in 2015 and was tipped for a long international career after former coach Duncan Fletcher likened him to Michael Vaughan. The following summer he played seven Tests against Sri Lanka and Pakistan and, although his scores were underwhelming (no half-century and an average of only 19.27), he performed better in the ODIs and T20Is against those sides. The following year his County Championship average was just 33 yet he was picked for that year's Ashes tour to Australia as selectors persisted with the view that he was the player to fill the awkward No. 3 berth, for which there were few obvious candidates.

Fast-forward to the first day of the first Test at the Gabba in Brisbane, where Pat Cummins is bowling and Vince is on 83. He's played some glorious shots, he's batted for four hours, and he's rescued England's day after Alastair Cook was out for 2. He's seen off two of the finest fast bowlers in the world in Cummins and Mitchell Starc, and the Aussies look distinctly crestfallen. A century beckons. Then Vince strokes the ball into the covers, where Nathan Lyon is patrolling, and calls captain Joe Root for a quick single. Lyon picks up one-handed, hurls the ball at the bowler's end and scores a direct hit on middle stump, leaving Vince two feet short of the crease. It was a magnificent piece of fielding by a player who, before the match started, had mischievously suggested that the series would end some English careers. Sadly, in the case of James Vince, he was proved right.

Looking back at that first Test, it strikes me that if Vince had completed his hundred it would have massively changed the tone of his career. Getting out to a direct hit is rare in Tests and the decision to run was reasonable, especially as he'd struck the shot well and Lyon had to move at full pace to pick up and throw. Vince just got unlucky. Former England opener Jonathan Trott once told me that a moment like that changes the narrative around a player. If you have an Ashes Test century under your belt, and in subsequent games the selectors are considering whether to drop you or someone else, that century will play on their minds. It may earn you another chance that otherwise wouldn't be forthcoming. They think: *Well, he's already done it once.*

Right place, right time

In women's cricket, Dani Hazell was a spinner I always felt deserved a longer run in the England team. She was part of our 2009 World Cup-winning squad but never played because in selection meetings she was always up against Laura Marsh and Holly Colvin. Our spin coach, Jack Birkenshaw, saw Laura as our biggest attacking threat and he was right: Laura ended up leading the wicket-taking charts in that tournament, with 16 victims at an average of 10.31, and over a 13-year career she took 217 international wickets across all three formats. Our other spinner was the left-armer Holly Colvin, whose stats weren't exactly shabby. She finished her eight-year England career with 174. Without those two, Dani would almost certainly have played many more games and plundered more wickets. Her stats were often slightly better than Laura's and Holly's but it wasn't until much later that she got a decent run in the side. Credit to her that she still finished with 146 wickets on the international stage. My own experience chimes with Dani's because I was trying to force my way into an England batting line-up that included Charlotte Edwards, Claire Taylor and Sarah Taylor, three of the best players in the world. It was almost impossible to knock them off their spot.

Being in the right place at the right time is a key component of luck – in cricket as in life – and Holly has the backstory to prove it. In 2005 she was showing promise but, as a 15-year-old kid, was never seriously in line for an England cap. In August 2005, the women's team coach Richard Bates invited her to a nets session at Hove County Cricket Ground, where England were preparing to face Australia. Richard knew the Aussies would be fielding their canny left-arm spinner Shelley Nitschke and reasoned that Holly's action would be similar, providing useful practice. After watching Holly, he asked her to be available for the upcoming four-day game, believing the Hove wicket would be spin-friendly. On 9 August 2005, aged 15 years and 336 days, she became the youngest cricketer of either sex to represent England. She proceeded to take two wickets in two balls and only narrowly missed a hat-trick. Later she admitted: 'I was fortunate . . . all these big names that were coming up against me – I had pretty much no idea.'

One-cap wonders

English Test history is awash with players who managed just one cap for their country. Sometimes this was down to monumental incompetence from selectors, or perhaps the result of a long lunch, but many a debutant has been thrown to the wolves without ever getting a chance to properly prove themselves. In the incompetence category, a leaf through nineteenth-century Test sides throws up some hilarious examples; who can forget Francis Alexander MacKinnon, the 35th MacKinnon of MacKinnon, whose length of time at the crease over two innings in Melbourne during the 1879 Ashes series was not dissimilar to the time it takes to say his name (he scored 0 and 5). MacKinnon was shuffled back to first-class cricket, where his pitiful performance as a batter (average 16.42 over ten years) resumed. He made one, distinctive mark in the annals by being second man out in the first ever Test hat-trick – achieved by the Aussies' demon pace bowler Fred Spofforth in that Melbourne match.

At least MacKinnon had played first-class cricket – unlike Joseph McMaster, picked for one Test during the 1988–9 series against South Africa. McMaster is unique in that he is the only player whose Test and first-class career consists of a single match. He didn't score a run, bowl, take a wicket or hold a catch. But everyone said he fielded well. Plus, he was a nice chap educated at Harrow.

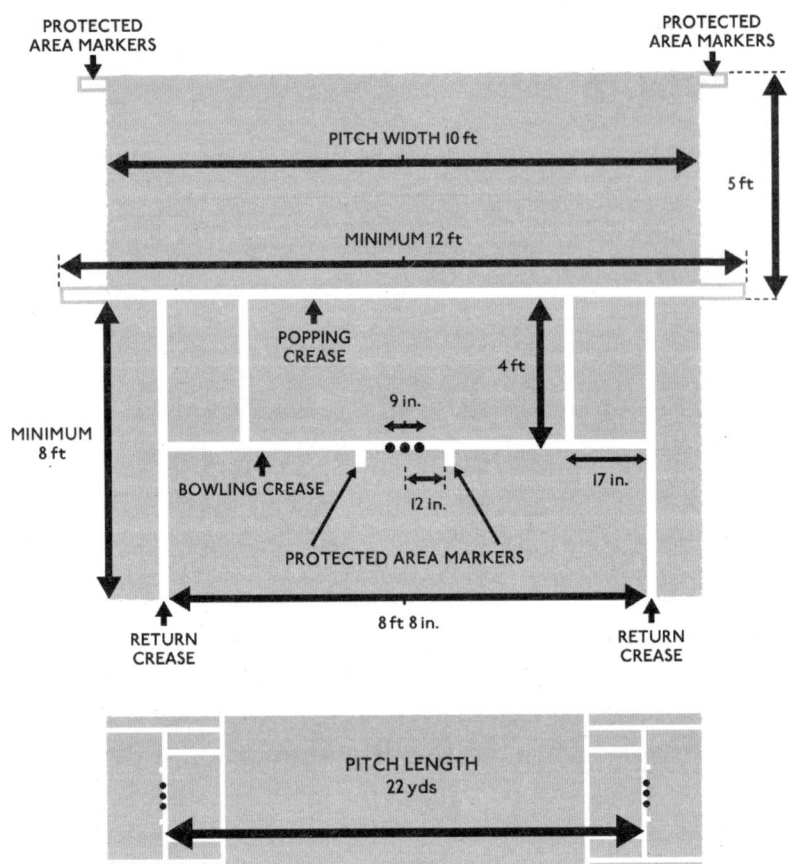

Ground

Let's start with the stumps, pitch and infield dimensions and markings (see illustration). They all have a specific purpose, but how they govern play in practice can be confusing even for club cricketers and, dare I say, the odd pro.

Three stumps Standing at each end of the playing strip, the stumps (together known as the wicket) occupy a space 9 in. wide and 28 in. high. Maximum stump diameter is 1.5 in. and the minimum 1.38 in. (see illustration on page 77).

Two bails These sit on top of the stumps, aka wicket. They are each 4.31 in. long and must project no more than half an inch above the stumps. At least one bail must be displaced for a batter to be out bowled. Bails traditionally comprise a 'barrel', a 'long spigot' and a 'short spigot'. But let's move on.

The pitch The pitch is 10 ft wide and extends 22 yds between each set of stumps. Confusingly, the pitch is also known as the wicket.

The bowling crease Marked in line with the stumps and centred on them, it runs for 8 ft 8 in. and indicates the end of the pitch.

- **The popping crease** In practice, we're talking here about the back edge of the popping crease, in other words the edge closest to the stumps. This is important because a batter whose foot or bat is *on* the crease, but not grounded *behind* it, can be stumped or run out. The bowler meanwhile must make sure some part of her front foot, whether grounded or raised, must be behind the popping crease in the delivery stride. The crease is 4 ft away from the stumps and a minimum 6 ft either side of middle stump. In practice, it is unlimited in length. Why is it called the popping crease? Supposedly something to do with popping holes, which featured in early versions of cricket. The batter had to pop their bat into the hole to avoid getting run out, while fielders had to pop the ball into it to achieve that very result. It was axed in favour of a crease – probably to avoid broken fingers.
- **The return creases** Each crease runs at right angles to the bowling and popping creases on either side of the wicket – each one measuring 4 ft 4 in. from middle stump. The bowler's back foot must land within, and not touching, a return crease.
- **The wide guidelines** Used only in limited-overs games, they help umpires enforce a much stricter definition of a wide. They run parallel with, and are 17 in. closer to, the stumps than the return creases.
- **The protected area** This is an area 5 ft by 12 ft immediately in front of the popping crease. There are indicator marks on the side furthest from the stumps. Woe betide bowlers who follow through a little too centrally – accidentally, of course – or fielders who wander onto it unnecessarily. Any roughing up of the protected area could help a bowler spin or seam the ball.

The infield circle Confined to limited-overs games. The infield comprises two semi-circles centred on each middle stump and extending 30 yds out. The semi-circles are joined by a dotted line running across the centre of the pitch. The circle restricts how many fielders can be assigned to protect boundaries (see P for Powerplay).

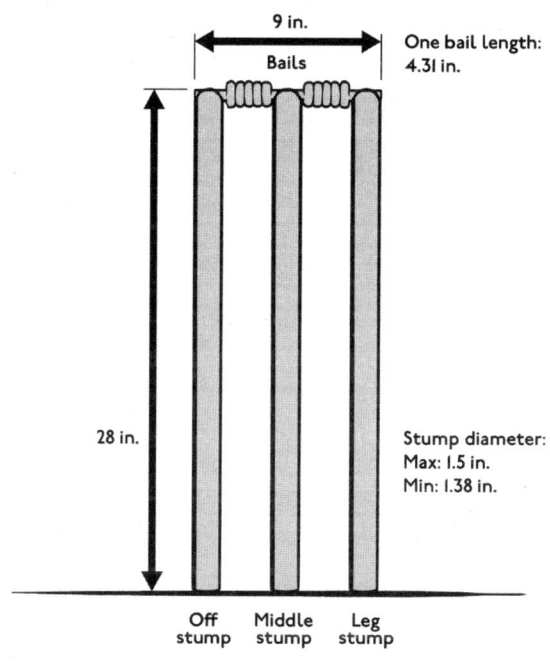

In the early days of women's cricket, we didn't get to play at The Oval or well-manicured private school grounds. We didn't even get covered wickets. We were assigned pitches ranging from a sodden 'sticky dog' to a ball-popping dust track. You could rarely rely on a ball doing what it should, based on its line and pitch, but this was an era where the mantra was 'suck it up and get on with it'. Later, my cricket apprenticeship proved valuable because when they did finally let me loose on The Oval pitches it felt like I'd died and gone to batter's heaven. My batting average (the number you get by dividing the number of runs you've scored by the number of times you've got out) soared above 60. It was wonderful. All international and county sides, and most higher league clubs, will try to prepare pitches suited to their strengths. At Surrey we generally tried to produce fast strips offering something to both batters and bowlers.

International selections for overseas tours are necessarily influenced by the anticipated ground conditions. Tours to India or Pakistan mean dry, dusty pitches that will help spin, and so spinners need to be first on the list. In English conditions you're looking at seamers and swing bowlers able to take advantage of moisture in the wicket. On the fastest pitches, usually Australian, genuinely quick bowlers are a boon. You need batters with a track record of playing well in the expected conditions – not just players in form – and you must decide the style of batting you want to adopt. If pitches are likely to wear quickly then it makes sense for Nos 1 to 4 to be dynamic batters who will cash in before the surface starts to go, which in limited-overs cricket usually means after the Powerplay. Finally, you look at the opposition: what are their main strengths and weaknesses? Are you a bit light on batting or is it worth picking an extra bowler? This is where a couple of seriously good all-rounders add steel and depth to a squad, whatever the pitch variables.

Drop-in pitches and lessons learned

Drop-in pitches are prepared by specialist curators away from the venue where they'll be used. I was in New York for the 2024 Men's World Cup where four had been flown in from

Adelaide and installed at a temporary stadium in Nassau County. I'm in favour of them as long as they're good-quality surfaces with consistent bounce. They bring live cricket to places where there's no established venue and open the game to a wider audience. US fans packed into the Nassau stadium and created a brilliant atmosphere, but the challenge for players was that those four pitches hadn't been given enough time to bed in. The turf should have had 12–18 months to adapt to the underlying soil and drainage and been tested regularly in the run-up to the tournament. Neither of those things happened and the result was cricket's equivalent of carnage. The pitches arrived barely six months before the first game. You could see lines between the various sections, and balls pitching in those areas popped and grubbed to the point that it felt dangerous. Teams used to scoring upwards of 220 in T20I competitions were getting skittled for around 100 and, while bowlers were no doubt delighted, batters were decidedly nervous. The former England captain Michael Vaughan summed it up when he posted on X: 'Trying to sell the game in the States is great – love it – but . . . this sub-standard surface in New York is unacceptable. You work so hard to make it to the WC, then have to play on this.' Despite all the criticism, the ICC later ruled that six of the eight matches were played on 'satisfactory' pitches, with only two – India v Ireland and Sri Lanka v South Africa – fought out on 'unsatisfactory' tracks. But the stats tell a more nuanced story. Those eight New York games produced an average first-innings score of 107.6. The long-term average in all T20Is is upwards of 160. Lessons will hopefully be learned, and for me it was another reminder of just how important groundsmen and women are to our national summer game. Most people have no conception of the hard graft that goes into producing a decent pitch.

Howzat

Howzat, or 'How's that', is the traditional appeal bellowed at an umpire when a fielding side believes a batter is out for any reason other than bowled (most cricket dismissals require an appeal). There are a few variations, such as 'Howizee', or 'How Is He', in men's games, while those of a more genteel nature sometimes avoid shouting altogether. I once heard a well-brought-up elderly bowler appeal for lbw by enquiring politely: 'Umpire?' The official assumed this was an appeal, although he could have been forgiven for responding: 'Yes, what?' Politeness didn't help in that instance; the appeal was rejected, perhaps due to lack of conviction.

For much of cricket's history the decision as to whether a batter was out depended entirely on the naked eye of an unbiased umpire. However, everything changed after the Decision Review System was launched in 2008 during a Test between Sri Lanka and India (see A for Actions). The DRS uses a suite of technological aids to help both on-field umpires, and an off-field third umpire, accurately rule on dismissals along with other potential areas of dispute such as no-balls and the validity of boundaries. It has unquestionably made the game fairer, added an element of tension and excitement for watching fans and is simple to understand.

There are two DRS systems in international cricket, Hawk-Eye and Virtual Eye, and they operate in similar ways. Multiple high-resolution cameras recording from different angles simultaneously track the centre of the ball in flight. If the batter gets in the way, and the ball doesn't hit bat or glove, the tracking software will show where it bounced and whether it would have hit the stumps – key elements governing an lbw appeal. The system is backed by slow-motion replays and, in the event of a disputed slip or wicket-keeper catch, the Snickometer, which uses directional microphones to detect the thinnest of contacts between bat and ball. 'Snicko', as it is affectionately known (affectionately to bowlers, at least), translates any faint noise onto a digital graph that is then synchronised with slow-motion footage to show the exact moment a ball passed, or touched, the bat. In real time, this is all played out in fractions of a second.

Going upstairs

The fielding captain and both batters have the right to refer disputed dismissals and rejected appeals to the third umpire – the DRS process known colloquially as 'going upstairs'. Players signal this by making a T-shape between their forearms, and from that point on everyone in the ground and those watching on TV can hear the third umpire deliberating on his assessment of ball tracking, slow-motion footage and sound-detection evidence. Players can ask for any dismissal to be reviewed, although they are limited to three unsuccessful reviews in Test matches and two during ODIs and T20s. Umpires can ask for a third umpire ruling in the case of marginal decisions, such as whether a low catch was pouched before it hit the ground, whether a batter made his ground during a run-out or stumping, whether a delivery was a no-ball or whether a fielder touched the boundary marker while in contact with the ball.

The only decision an umpire *cannot* refer upstairs is lbw, which must initially be decided on the field. It's up to the batters or fielding captain to call for a review if they think the on-field official is wrong and, if that happens, proceedings may be subject to an additional frisson of tension. Let's say the fielding side is convinced a batter is out lbw. The umpire agrees and raises a finger. But the batter thinks a 'clear mistake' has been made and goes upstairs, leaving the third umpire to decide whether any one of five scenarios should overturn the dismissal. These are:

(a) The ball pitched outside the line of leg stump.
(b) The ball hit the bat before hitting a pad.
(c) The ball failed to hit the pad in line with the stumps (however, a batter can still be out lbw if she failed to play a genuine shot to a ball pitching outside off stump).
(d) It was a no-ball.
(e) Ball tracking shows that the ball would have gone on to miss the stumps.

It is that 'e' scenario that could prove so agonising for a reviewing batter. If any part of the ball is hitting the stumps, it's not a clear mistake and so the dismissal becomes 'umpire's call'. In other words, the batter is out. Conversely, had the on-field umpire given the batter *not out*, and the fielding captain had reviewed, the batter would have stayed put because, again, no clear mistake was evident. Importantly, if a decision comes down to umpire's call, the team that went upstairs doesn't lose a review.

There are times when the whole process makes you cringe; you see batters demanding a review for a catch behind when they know they snicked it – and the keeper, slips and dogs on the street know it – and the umpire immediately raises the finger. That said, if their team's innings is nearing the end, what's there to lose? There are also tactical uses of DRS reviews by the fielding side. They might want to slow the game down or illustrate to the umpire that a not-out decision was a mere whisker away from being out – an attempt to swing the next marginal decision in their favour. These are nuances in a game and they aren't always obvious to spectators.

Although the DRS hasn't eliminated controversies (see Virender Sehwag's dismissal in A for Actions), the most glaring errors have largely disappeared from the international game. Away from the elite level, however, there remains an art to appealing. In my view, there must be sufficient conviction to persuade the umpire that she simply *has* to raise her finger. That means direct eye contact and trusting your wicket-keeper to join in. If it's only you screaming 'howzat', the umpire may think you're at best hopelessly optimistic and at worst desperate. There's also the risk of over-appealing, which rarely goes down well, or wildly celebrating before the umpire has even made a decision (umpires hate that).

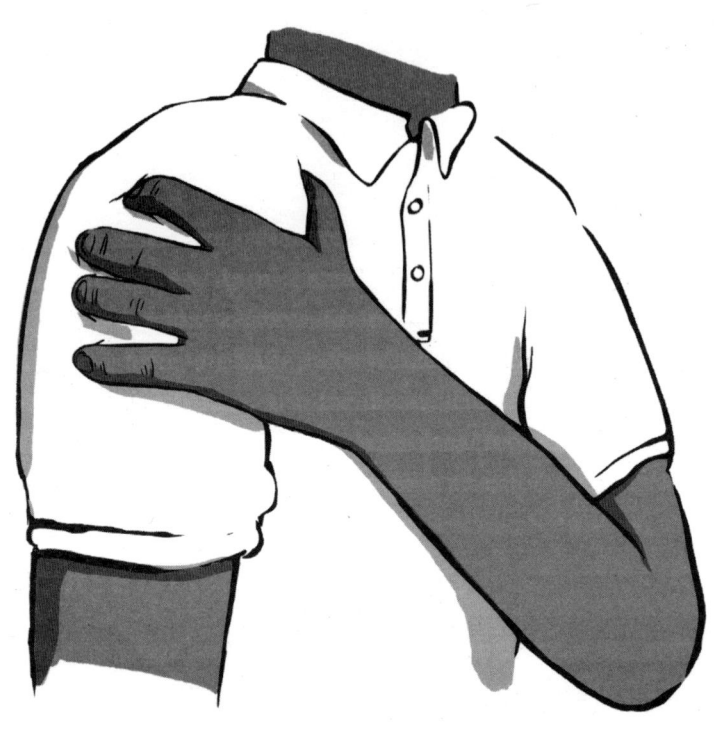

Injury

Short-term injuries are frustrating but there's often a lot you can do in terms of physio and gym work to get back in business quickly. Long-term injuries are a different beast because they scramble your thoughts and wear you down mentally. When I suffered the worst of my back breakdowns I couldn't walk properly for a year and was out of cricket for three years. It happened at an England squad camp in Guildford run by Richard Bates – the coach who helped us regain the Ashes in 2005. I was aged 19 and on the fringe of things, but he called me down to bowl at Lottie and some of the senior players. I drove up in my red Ford Fiesta, so excited, feeling on top of the world and then, fourth ball, I suddenly felt this sharp back pain. It was horrible. I didn't even explain properly to Richard. I just said: 'Sorry, I have to leave,' drove home, got inside, bent down to pick up the TV remote and I was out, immobile on the floor in agony.

I was told by a doctor around that time that I might not play cricket again and that I could have issues with paralysis. That's a big fear for a teenager to manage. Was everything I'd worked for going to be taken away? Would I ever be able to bowl again? Could I even get fit enough to train? And could

I truly trust my body when it came to the crunch? I had sustained two prolapsed discs and a pars defect, which is where the upper and lower sections of the vertebrae become separated due to repeated stress and strain. I also had a fracture, known as spondylolisthesis, in the lower one. You can get this from bowling and I had my dodgy action from a young age, which must have caused wear and tear. But there's also a known genetic link and, in my case, they couldn't be certain of the cause. There was an option to operate, inserting pins to strengthen the bones, but I decided against that. I still do exercises to keep my back healthy.

Fortunately, I was introduced to a rehab model created by the former British athletics star Kriss Akabusi. It was called the Cycle of Renewal and it began with an objective explanation of what happens mentally when you're unable to do the thing you love. In essence, when you're down like that, the quality of the questions you ask yourself affects how quickly you'll recover. Typically, you start by wallowing in self-pity: 'Why did it have to happen to me?' Or: 'Will I ever come back from this?' Or: 'If I do get back playing for England, will I be as good?' It's a dark place. The point when things change for the better is when an athlete starts asking the right questions and setting goals.

When I got injured, I set myself the goal of being part of England's 2009 World Cup squad. I wrote that on a piece of paper and stuck it on my fridge so that I looked at it every day. And every day I would visualise that goal and ask myself what I had to do *that day* to achieve it. This was my driver. It demanded a clear plan and it required me to do the rounds of the specialists and the physios and condemn myself to the godforsaken, impossibly boring rehab work. When it got unbearably hard, I'd fall back on my driver-goal and my

Injury

team-mates. Getting a call from Isa Guha or Caroline Atkins on the lines of 'mate, we miss you, we want you back' gave me an incredible lift because it meant I wasn't alone in this struggle. I also took inspiration from others who'd been through the injury mill, such as Katherine Sciver-Brunt. She'd had so many back operations. I got my first England cap because she broke down injured, but she gradually fought back and her very first ball on her return to competitive cricket was a vicious, fast bouncer. To have that faith in herself, to risk her body straight away, was great to see and it helped me put aside all the niggling fears about whether I'd still be the player I was. Katherine parked her fear and moved on. I was determined to do the same – and, thankfully, I did.

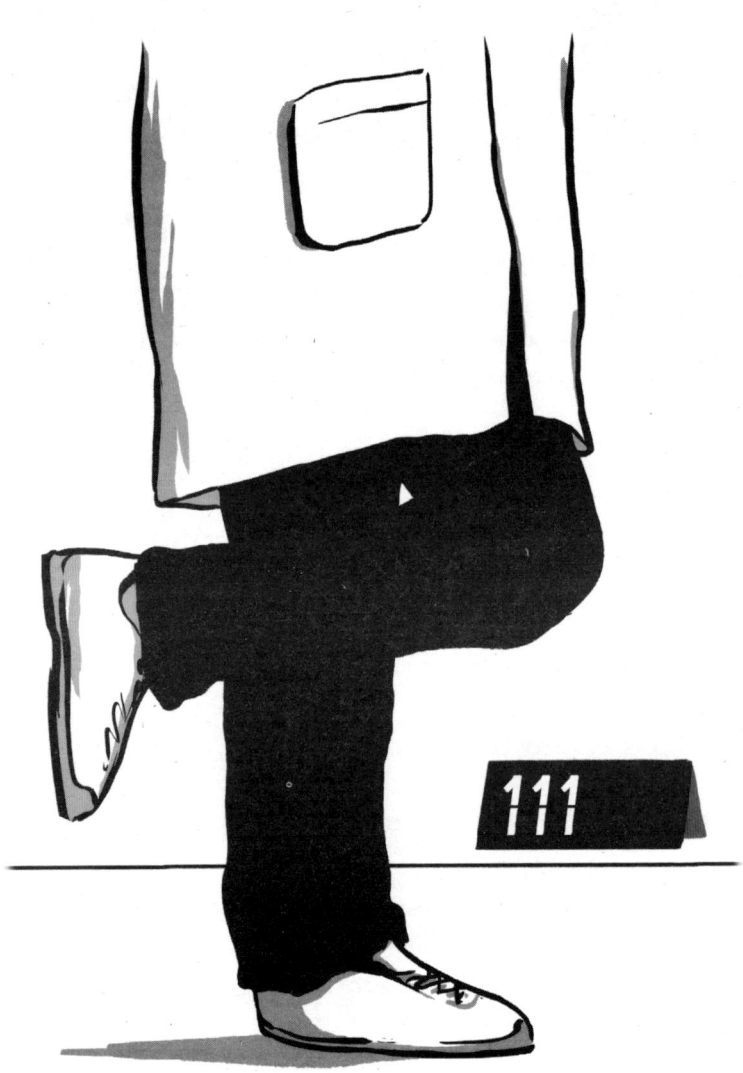

J

Jinxes

Everyone had a routine in the dressing room. Before a game I always had to put my left pad on before my right. Same with my boots and gloves. If I wasn't sure or couldn't remember whether I'd followed this rule, I would take everything off and start again. If that sounds obsessive, it got worse out in the middle. I had a slightly staggered guard for which I would *reverse* my left-then-right rule. So, when taking up position, it was always right foot before left. On the odd occasion I got that wrong I would have to walk out to square leg before trying again. If I got out early, I'd be walking back to the pavilion, shaking my head, wondering if the *real* reason was that I'd somehow not followed these rituals. Call it superstition, confirmation bias, whatever you want, but I convinced myself that if I strayed from the correct order of things it would produce bad energy. Maybe it was a way of focusing on the task ahead. Or processing failure when things went wrong.

Sometimes I'd arrive at a ground and, regardless of whether I'd played there before, I'd get a bad vibe for no obvious reason. I'd tell myself I wasn't going to get any runs. There are cognitive tools that sports psychologists now teach to cope with negative thinking or poor concentration – things like wearing a wristband that you snap to reset yourself and switch on. One of my few regrets is that sports psychology was still emerging when I was a young player. It would have helped a lot.

Superstitions

My left-then-right thing is probably rooted in the notion that you must always walk right for runs and left for wickets. That was drilled into me from the age of 12. It's a non-negotiable superstition, I've always abided by it and every international team I ever played knew the same rule. In my time, if any England player was spotted walking left when they should have been walking right, their team-mates would raise merry hell. It works like this: if your team is batting, but you're not out in the middle yourself, you might fancy a stroll around the boundary to watch the bowlers from different angles. Or perhaps you've got out early and need to get away from your mates for a boundary walk to avoid exposing them to your negative thoughts. Whatever, make sure you walk to the right from your starting point because right means runs.

This is all superstitious stuff and nonsense that made absolutely no difference to our fortunes in a game. We obviously had no statistical evidence to bear it out, yet we convinced ourselves it worked and so, in a subconscious way, it did. It placed us in the right mindset and kept us focused on proceedings. Even as a commentator, I still walk the right way around the boundary if I'm doing interviews on the outfield.

In cricket there's an argument that superstition and psychology are two sides of the same coin. Cricketers are quite capable of creating a superstition based on nothing at all. Then, when everyone in the game hears about it and runs with it, it becomes a kind of psychological weapon to wield against your opponents – even though it's a blatant load of tosh. Take the recent examples of bowlers swapping over the bails on a set of stumps. Who knows quite where this started but it came to prominence in the 2019 Ashes when Australia off-spinner Nathan Lyon indulged in a spot of bails-twiddling during the fourth Test at Old Trafford. England were cruising at 163 for two thanks to a 138-run partnership between Rory Burns and Joe Root when Root spotted that Lyon had flipped the bails at the non-striker's end. Root promptly flipped them back, not that it helped. Burns scored only two more runs and Root just three. Stuart Broad, who was playing in that match, then copied the stunt at The Oval in the 2023 Ashes as England desperately sought a breakthrough with Australia on 91 for one. Marnus Labuschagne edged the very next delivery from Mark Wood, Root took a belting catch at slip and Broad – bizarrely, he later admitted – rushed to celebrate with Aussie non-striker Usman Khawaja. Khawaja was in no mood for hugging, tartly informing Broad: 'If you touch my bails I'm flipping them straight back.' Broad explained later: 'I've heard it's an Aussie change-of-luck thing.' Five months later it was India's Virat Kohli who invoked the curse of the bail-flip. He tried it on day two of the first Test against South Africa as the hosts' Dean Elgar and Tony de Zorzi motored along at five runs per over. It took only six more balls before de Zorzi was out caught, then new batter Keegan Petersen was bowled the following over. On such evidence are new jinxes born.

Don't eat duck

For many years in the 1980s and 1990s the England Men's dressing room clung to the notion that you should never eat duck on the eve of a game. This perhaps says more about a penchant for fine dining than any risk of tempting fate, but there is at least a soupçon more to this than simply the word 'duck'. The story goes that at close of play on the fourth day of the 1982 Lord's Test against Pakistan, England were in a parlous position. They needed a single run to avoid the follow-on (see glossary) but the last man in was Robin Jackman, a good bowler but not a player renowned for his batting tenacity. To take Jackman's mind off the responsibility resting on his shoulders, team-mates David Gower and Allan Lamb suggested that the three of them should dine that evening at a reputable French restaurant. All three ordered duck, and the seeds of destruction were sown. The following day Jackman was immediately out lbw to Imran Khan for a duck and, after England followed on, medium-pacer Mudassar Nazar dismissed both Lamb and Gower, also for ducks. The hosts were thrashed by ten wickets. Why, oh why, didn't that foolish trio just plump for fish and chips?

Nelson's curse

Cricket is a numbers game and so it would be unconscionable not to mention the two best-known 'cursed' numbers: 111 for England and 87 for Australia. There are several competing theories as to why 111 has become known as a Nelson. One is that it stands for Admiral Horatio Nelson's 'one eye, one arm and one leg', although since Nelson never lost a leg or an eye (he lost sight in one eye) this feels a bit research-light. Another has it that 111 refers to Nelson's three great naval triumphs – the Nile (1798), Copenhagen (1801) and Trafalgar (1805) – but it doesn't much sound like bad luck proved a gamechanger for the Admiral on any of those

Jinxes

occasions. A third view is that 111 looks like a set of stumps minus the bails so, er, nothing to do with Nelson then. An analysis by *The Cricketer* magazine during the 1990s found that in terms of statistical significance, English wickets were no more likely to fall on 111 than on any other number. Unsurprisingly perhaps, most wickets fell on 0. Nevertheless, there's no denying that cricket has bought into this particular superstition – also invoked whenever a score hits a double Nelson (222) or a triple Nelson (333). English umpire David Shepherd would stand or hop on one leg if 111 appeared on the scoreboard, much to the glee of TV directors, but the most remarkable example of the Nelson effect came on 11 November 2011 as South Africa headed for victory in the first Cape Town Test against Australia. At precisely 11.11am, with the scoreboard reading 11:11 11/11/11, and South Africa needing 111 to win, most of the crowd joined English umpire Ian Gould in a Shepherd-style one-legged stance until the relevant minute was up. I've no idea what kind of Nelson that was, but some club scorer, somewhere, will know or at least be able to offer a credible suggestion.

And so we come to number 87, known as the Devil's Number among Aussies, on the basis that it is 13 runs short of a coveted century. (Curiously, having the *actual* number 13 on the scoreboard doesn't seem to worry them so much.) This jinx stems from a belief held by the great Australian all-rounder Keith Miller (see F for Form) who, as a ten-year-old boy, was so stunned to see his hero Don Bradman bowled for 87 while playing for New South Wales in a Sheffield Shield game at the Melbourne Cricket Ground in 1929, that he began combing through newspaper scorecards to find further evidence of the 87 'curse'. Miller would voice his fear to anyone who would listen and, when commentators such as Richie Benaud and

How to Read Cricket

Alan Davidson picked up on his theory, it adopted a life of its own. The Aussie legend decided he'd better do some fact-checking, obtained a copy of the scorebook from that MCG game and discovered the inconvenient truth that Bradman had got out on 89. Miller blamed the Melbourne scoreboard operators for being late in advancing Bradman's score. It was certainly too late to backtrack. Australia were condemned to be forever dogged by the curse of 87.

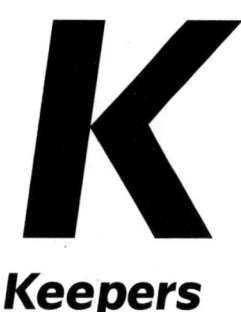

Keepers

It's a foolish bowler who doesn't cultivate a good relationship with her wicket-keeper. A keeper's role goes much further than stopping wayward deliveries run away for four – she acts both as your trusted adviser and your spy. She can tell if something's awry in your action; perhaps your upper body position is falling away instead of staying upright. She can spot changes in a batter's strategy that you may not have noticed, such as a subtly different guard or a stance further out from the crease. She can initially set and adjust your slip cordon because she's best placed to judge the speed and bounce of the ball off the wicket. Above all, she can support you in any lbw or slip-catch appeal and advise on whether it's worth referring a not-out on-field decision to the third umpire. A bowler doesn't always see or hear a faint nick behind, but the keeper almost always knows.

I bowled to many brilliant ones over the years but if I had to pick my favourite it would be Sarah Taylor, who always made me look good even when I hurled down an absolute shocker. Her hands were so quick and her intuition so polished – almost a sixth sense – that she could make it seem like we'd hatched a plan for me to bowl two yards outside off stump. She cleaned up everything, including erratic throw-ins from fielders, although she was also good at laser stares if you were way off the mark.

That Bairstow stumping

I love a bit of drama on a cricket field. So when Australia's wicket-keeper Alex Carey stumped England wicket-keeper Jonny Bairstow moments before lunch on the fifth day of the second Ashes Test at Lord's in July 2023, it was box-office telly as far as I was concerned. No sign of a wicket-keepers' union here. Cameron Green had just bowled the sixth ball of the 52nd over – not the same thing as the *end* of that over – an innocuous slow bouncer that Bairstow ducked under. Carey, standing some 20 yards back, collected the ball on the bounce and in the same action threw it underarm straight back at Bairstow's stumps. Replays showed Carey hadn't waited for Bairstow to walk out of his crease; he merely thought it was worth a pop on the off-chance he might. And Carey wasn't disappointed. With the ball still in mid-air, and without so much as a glance behind, Bairstow headed off down the pitch to chat with his captain Ben Stokes. He was a yard out of his ground as the ball cannoned into the stumps. Later he would claim it was obvious he wasn't seeking a cheeky run because he'd tapped his bat and scratched his boot inside the crease, indicating he thought the ball was 'dead'.

Law 20 gives several scenarios where the ball can be considered dead. One is when it is 'finally settled' in the hands of the wicket-keeper, which it clearly wasn't here. Another is when the bowler's end umpire (in this case Ahsan Raza) concludes that the fielding side and both batters have 'ceased to regard it as in play', but the Aussies regarded it as still very much in play. Running out batters with a direct hit on the stumps is cricket's equivalent of gold dust, which is why they all rushed to congratulate Carey. Later, Stokes said he would have withdrawn the stumping appeal if he'd been in the position of Australia captain Pat Cummins. Of course, it would have been OK to do that, but it's ridiculous to suggest that – just because Cummins took a different view (a view that complied with the Laws of Cricket) – somehow Australia were guilty of an underhand, unsporting act. If Carey had been standing up to the stumps for a slow bowler, Bairstow would have stayed put. He's not a casual player but here he was guilty of a casual act – and not for the first time in this series. The Aussies had noted it and, fair play to them, it was entirely his fault that he lost his wicket.

L

Leadership

At the end of my first overseas tour, that 2006–7 quadrangular tournament in Chennai, our skipper Lottie Edwards laid into us in the dressing room. It was a proper shouty-sweary rollicking, and rightly so because we'd been battered by everyone. The final table read New Zealand 21 points, Australia 18, India 13, England 0, although we did win the third-place play-off against India to recover some pride. In the changing room it wasn't pretty. What were we doing this for? Why all the effort if we end up being crap? We were representing our country. We should never forget why we're here. And then someone in the corner quietly began singing the chorus of an old Take That song, 'Never Forget', which begins: 'Never forget where you've come here from'. And then everyone was singing it over and over. Very loudly. That day we decided it would be our theme tune, we would sing it on the bus heading to matches, and when we won we'd be screaming it at full volume in the dressing room – dancing around, jumping on tables. Soon we were putting together our amazing winning run, and a couple of years later we were double world champions. I'm not saying Lottie's broadside, or us singing Take That, was the secret. The entire England women's set-up went through a complete rebuild after Chennai, with new coaches, new backroom staff, the lot. But there's no doubt that the song anchored us. It was a team ritual and actually *did* remind us where we'd come from and of the desire to perform for our country, our families and our fans. For me, it meant thinking about my mum and Jenny Wostrack and others who had sacrificed things for me so that I could become a professional cricketer. It was humbling.

Cricket, mind, is a fickle creature. You think you've cracked it – you've run the hard miles, honed your skills, got a great team spirit – and then suddenly the cricket gods decide you're getting too big for your boots. That was us in the Caribbean in 2009. We'd just won two World Cups and retained the Ashes, but in the West Indies it all fell apart. We played matches on Saint Kitts in small grounds with big, lairy crowds and they just got stuck into us in every sense. I had people telling me: 'You don't even know what country you're from. What's wrong with you?' We were beaten 2–1 in the three-match ODI series and 2–1 in the T20 games. After one humiliation it was carnage in the dressing room – bats flying around, players crying, coaches trying to restore calm and order. In some ways it wasn't a bad thing because it showed we cared. We had been rattled by an up-and-coming team in a year where we'd proved we were the best in the world. We came away from that series with tension in the camp and it fed through to our next tour in India four months later. Had we put too much pressure on ourselves – obsessed with winning rather than remembering where we'd come from, and focusing on our own performances? We went from a united changing room to one that started separating into little cliques. I went into one with the two Dannis – Hazell and Wyatt-Hodge – to disappear and try to get away from the madness. It was an interesting experience to go from an amazing changing room to a dark one, where no one was really getting on. We lost the India ODI series 3–2 but we did eventually pull together and restored some self-respect by winning the three T20 matches 2–1.

Staying focused

When I became captain of Surrey Women, part of the job involved giving motivational pre-match team talks. My early efforts dropped like lead balloons. I would get overly hyped up and excited. Even when I thought I'd been inspirational and that I'd landed something with the girls, I'd finish to the sound of silence and then someone – usually Cecily Scutt – would say: 'Ebz, chill out. It's a game of cricket.' I had to learn how to read the team, read the moment and understand that my main task as captain was to cultivate calm and keep my team focused. The best players don't need or want to be revved up.

I captained Surrey for about five years. When I was appointed, we were an under-performing side despite being one of the bigger counties, and so the highlight of my tenure was getting us into Division 1. Unfortunately, the glory vanished like autumn mist and we dropped back down the following season. I was a reluctant captain because I didn't like the additional expectations that came with it. I got the job because I was the best player, I played for England and I scored lots of runs. None of which proved I was destined to be a great captain. It didn't mean I instantly switched on as a tactician because, as a player, I never thought too hard about what was happening during a game. We were either winning or losing. Once I was in charge, I had to take field settings much more seriously. Where did the batter place risky shots? How could we place fielders to make her take more risks? With experienced bowlers this was easy – they knew exactly what was needed because they'd bowled dozens of overs at the opponent facing them. But for the younger ones, perhaps nervous and feeling they were on trial, I needed to get more involved. I'd ruminate over fielding positions and tell them to focus on their bowling. I may have been light on tactical nous but I do think I had empathy with my players and knew what motivated them. I didn't want to be one of those naturally talented captains who couldn't understand why everyone wasn't similarly blessed.

One of the hardest things about cricket is the subjectivity of the selection process. Against certain teams you might decide, for tactical reasons, that you need a different No. 3 or 4. You 'feel' a certain player is right for that position. But 'feel' is not objective. Another senior pro could construct an equally cogent argument for 'feeling' someone else would be better. You can look at stats all you like but the differences they show are often marginal and, before you know it, you're going round in circles agonising over who's right. I was fortunate to have Jeremy Greaves as a coach throughout my time at Surrey and we'd keep selection meetings tight – just me and him – to avoid too many voices in the mix. You'd come out of those conflabs and have to explain to a player that she hadn't made the cut for an upcoming game – always a delicate conversation. She might decide that this amounts to a loss of faith. To borrow a cricketing analogy cherished by politicians, you need to 'roll the pitch' – lowering expectations in advance of a selection meeting but also remaining positive about a future return to the team.

If I saw a player struggling for form I'd spend time with them, find out what was going on, try to unpick the issue and establish whether it was a technical thing or a state of mind. Disenchanted players do no one any favours, least of all a captain, because negativity spreads fast and suddenly you're the bad guy holding back their career. As captain, your best defence against criticism is obviously to hit lots of runs and win matches, but a couple of personal low scores or team thrashings quickly jack up the pressure. You're meant to be leading and you're not doing your job. Maybe you've been tactically naive or haven't responded quickly to a fast-moving match situation, preferring instead to stick to your stock plan.

Triumph and disaster

The best captains are intuitive. They see a potential problem before it takes hold, whereas others – and I'd include myself here – become too reactive. This is where you need feedback from a good coach. Jeremy would take me to one side and point out key moments where decisions I'd made had cost us dear. Perhaps my emotions had taken over, or I'd become obsessed with pursuing a failing game plan. Such exchanges would never happen within earshot of players. Do that and it's game over. Overall, I'd say captaincy improved me as a player because it made me more focused. I loved to bat creatively, which meant I sometimes got out in silly ways while trying some ludicrously funky shot. The moment I felt others relying on me, I tightened my game. I had to set the tone and show how much I valued my wicket. How could I roast a team-mate for getting out on a wild flash outside off stump when I'd just done pretty much exactly that myself?

There are many components to success as a cricket captain, but establishing a brand – a strategic overview that coaches and senior players can all embrace – is the foundation. If a team doesn't buy in to that then there's almost no point turning up. This is why, for me, Ben Stokes stands out as an international skipper. He's committed to attacking cricket and, while that won't always work, it does create clarity of purpose. He's also a stable character. I started as a bubbly, mouthy captain but I soon learned that what my players really wanted was calm in the face of battle. Someone focused on process rather than outcomes. To paraphrase Rudyard Kipling, a captain who can meet triumph and disaster and treat both those imposters just the same. I don't know whether I truly mastered the demands of captaincy, but I learned an awful lot along the way.

The difference between triumph and disaster also involves luck, and winning the toss sometimes feels massive. I always called tails. Changing your call every time on a whim seemed crazy to me because I suspected it messed with the odds. I've subsequently found out that, mathematically, this is not the case and that if a coin is tossed in precisely the same way on the same surface and lands heads-up on 99 consecutive occasions, the odds on the 100th coming up heads remain 50–50. It's also the case that statistically, over the long term, the toss conveys only a marginal advantage. Up to 2023, a Test match-winning toss resulted in a 36.7 per cent win rate in matches and a 31.8 per cent loss rate, although if you look only at recent years the toss advantage appears greater. There's no clear explanation for this, but one theory is that spinners have become more valuable since the adoption of DRS. This has produced more wickets for them given that umpires no longer feel they must give batters the benefit of the doubt. As spinners usually come into their own on a deteriorating fourth- or fifth-day pitch, captains are more inclined to bat first and leave their opponents the task of surviving the fourth innings of the match against a spinning ball. In ODIs the win–lose toss advantage is even smaller than Tests (48.2 per cent against 47.4 per cent), while in T20s it is a disadvantage statistically to call correctly: teams that win a T20 toss go on to win 47.6 per cent of matches, but teams that lose the toss win 48.4 per cent.

Captain Hindsights

I usually brought out my own coin, a £2 coin, to place in the umpire's hands, although it wasn't always accepted. Maybe they wanted to be seen as fiercely independent. In some ways, losing the toss is better than winning because if you're unsure whether to bat or bowl you're not condemning your team-mates to the consequences of your decision. The received wisdom – that if you win the toss you should bat – isn't compelling when you consider the empirical results data. Sometimes it's the obvious choice: the pitch looks like a road and the sun's out. But where there's a hint of green on a length, or some cloud cover, then if I call correctly, we're bowling. Often you don't know whether you've made the right decision until you've seen a few overs go through. Pundits and players talk about 'reading' the pitch, but who really knows? You might *pretend* you know because you need to sell your decision to your players. If it all goes wrong, if the opposition racks up 300 or you collapse to 30 for seven, you can be sure where the blame will be pinned: 'Ebony, mate, what did you do that for?'

This is why I sympathise greatly with Nasser Hussain,

who still hasn't shaken off the spectre of November 2003 and the first Ashes Test at 'Fortress Brisbane' when he won the toss and famously told a TV interviewer: 'We're gonna have a bowl.' By the time stumps were drawn that day, Australia were 364 for two and England would never recover in a series they eventually lost 4–1. Typically, Nasser fessed up like a true leader: 'It's obvious, blatantly obvious, that the decision I made to send Australia in to bat in the first Test was wrong,' he said later. 'As England captain, I am paid to make decisions and I am big enough to admit that this one was a big mistake.' But was it? For all those Captain Hindsights who condemned him, Nasser could not have foreseen that his main strike bowler, Simon Jones, would rupture his anterior cruciate ligament in the morning session. Nor that his fielders would ground a host of dropped chances. Aside from which, England were up against one of the all-time great Australian sides, a team that included Shane Warne, Glenn McGrath and Jason Gillespie, who had already amassed more than 1,000 Test wickets between them. Every batter in that Aussie top seven would finish his Test career averaging over 45, including three who averaged over 50. It's hardly surprising that, according to a computer-generated match simulation of that Brisbane Test, England had a 4 per cent chance of winning under Nasser's bowl-first strategy. But, guess what, they also had a 4 per cent chance of winning if they had batted first. Who'd be a captain?

M

Mind Games

Mind Games are everywhere in cricket. Sometimes they're subtle – perhaps a little distraction chat about the wearing pitch – but sometimes they take the brutal form of direct insults aimed at undermining a batter's confidence, a practice known as sledging. Sledging doesn't plumb the same depths in women's cricket as you occasionally see with the men. But it happens and it can get tasty – especially if you end up 'exchanging pleasantries' with England team-mates. On one occasion I was opening the batting for Surrey with Sarah Taylor wicket-keeping for Sussex and Caroline Atkins at first slip. Before we even got going, Caroline was giving me chat: 'The ball will swing loads today, girls, she's gonna snick one.' And sure enough, I did, first ball. Which Caroline dropped. Normally a batter stays out of verbals and just lets the fielding side chunter away, but I decided on some reverse-sledging: 'I did as predicted, Caroline, what went wrong?' She wasn't happy and it got worse because she dropped me again a few balls later, whereupon I may have questioned whether there was *any* danger of her catching one. At the end I offered her my hand, but she refused to shake it, saying I had undermined the spirit of cricket. What? She was the one who started sledging me!

Perhaps I should have followed the advice of occasional TMS summariser Alec Stewart, a Surrey colleague and giant of the English game, who had a quietly effective method of dealing with sledging: 'If a bowler had been giving me a mouthful at the start of my innings,' he told BBC Sport, 'and yet three hours later or so I was 80 not out, I might point out that they had gone a bit quiet. It was just a case of letting them know I had won that little battle.' Wise words. All I'd say is that if a game is too nice and polite then to me it's not sport. But you should always leave harsh words out on the field. Sarah and I made up, we're good friends and I'm proud that she chose me as a godparent to her child.

Love Hearts

The Aussies were always innovative when it came to mind games. Back in the 1990s they targeted one of our best batters, Barbara Daniels, by placing Love Hearts along the batting crease. As fans of these sweets well know, each one carries a short message that is sometimes romantic but can also refer to dumping someone. A player in the Aussie camp had obviously been sent out to buy up the entire stock of a sweetshop because, when Barbara went out to bat, she was greeted with a line of Love Hearts all bearing the same words: 'Bye-bye Barbara'.

Pre-match mind games

Long before anyone thought cricket data was a thing, bowlers would do their own back-of-a-fag-packet assessment of rookie batters and sometimes inform their intended victim of the result. The late, great, fire-breathing England fast bowler Fred Trueman, a former TMS commentator, had a habit of wandering into tourists' changing rooms on the morning of a Test match to let them know that balls would be bouncing around their chins: 'Can you hook, son,' he would enquire of the nerviest-looking youngster, 'cause you'll get the chance today.' His other mischievous habit while fielding would be to lurk around the boundary gate after a wicket fell. As the new batter opened it he'd hear Fred's gruff Yorkshire tones: 'Don't bother shutting it, son. You won't be out there long.'

My top three all-time great sledging exchanges

Sir Viv Richards v Greg Thomas

Sir Viv has always been a cricketing hero of mine. To retire with a Test average above 50 is an incredible achievement, and his ability to dismantle bowling attacks with flair and panache was a sight to behold. So who was the plucky bowler who decided to sledge the master in his prime? Step forward, Glamorgan paceman Greg Thomas in a match against Viv's adopted county of Somerset. Thomas – no mean cricketer himself – had tempted the Antiguan into several 'plays and misses' and decided to point this out: 'It's red, it's round and it weighs about five ounces,' said Thomas, 'now, try to hit it.' Viv said nothing but obliged by walloping the next ball out of the ground. Then he sauntered down the wicket to conclude the conversation: 'Greg, you know what it looks like. Now go and find it.'

Andrew Flintoff v Tino Best

To Lord's for the 2004 first Test against the West Indies. The tourists were in a doomed fourth-innings run chase with Shivnarine Chanderpaul the only recognised batter left as fast bowler Tino Best strode to the wicket. After seeing an unprepossessing swipe at a ball from England spinner Ashley Giles (Best missed by a country mile), a grinning Andrew Flintoff wandered up from slip with a cheeky request to 'mind the windows, Tino' (a reference to the upper tier of the Lord's Pavilion). A few balls later a fired-up Tino went for a second huge swing, missed again, got stumped and headed off with three to his name. Not all sledging needs to be nasty.

Jimmy Ormond v Mark Waugh

Leicestershire's Jimmy Ormond was no doubt expecting some stick when he arrived at the batting crease on his debut for England in the 2001 fifth Ashes Test against Australia at The Oval. He wasn't disappointed. Australia's Mark Waugh, who had scored 120 in the first innings, greeted him with the words: 'Look who it is. Mate, what are you doing out here? There's no way you're good enough to play for England.' Ormond stopped, gazed around the field and spotted Mark's brother, Aussie captain Steve Waugh (who had just scored 157). 'Maybe not,' he replied, 'but at least I'm the best player in my family.'

99

N

Nervous Nineties

Whenever my batting total entered the nervous nineties, it would mess with my head. I'd be panicking about the next few minutes – the future – rather than concentrating on the present. I sometimes became focused on the milestone rather than my game. In the big scheme of things, why does it matter? Ninety is a fantastic score. If you've posted that then you've almost certainly given your team a chance of victory. At Surrey, I worked for a while with Michael Carberry, a good friend and a formidable opening bat. He helped me deal with 'nineties angst' at a time when he was posting double hundreds in the county game. It came down to largely the same advice that governs all cricket skills: focus on the here and now. Don't overthink. Don't imbue your numbers with too much importance. It's the team that matters. Yet a three-figure score is what people remember – fans, team-mates, coaches, pundits, cricket stattos (especially stattos) – and in relatively short careers you want as many centuries as possible in the record books.

In ODIs, some of England's most celebrated batters have suffered the agonising fate of falling a run short: Ben Stokes in 2021 against India, Jos Buttler in 2014 against West Indies, and

Andrew Flintoff in 2004 against India. India's greatest batter of modern times, Sachin Tendulkar, even managed to post three 99 dismissals inside five months in 2007: ODIs against South Africa, England and Pakistan. As for England's Test batters, the last four decades have seen Marcus Trescothick, Michael Atherton and Graham Gooch all succumb on scores of 99, while England's Ian Bell is among only a dozen or so players, from all Test-playing nations, to fall on 199 since the turn of the twentieth century. You feel for all of them, but a special mention has to go to New Zealand's Martin Crowe, out for 299 against Sri Lanka in 1991 after more than ten hours at the crease, and Alex Tudor of Surrey and England. Tudes is in a slightly different category in that his landmark Test score was 99 not out. The reason he didn't complete his century at Edgbaston on 3 July 1999 was because England beat New Zealand before he could. But that's only half the story. As a 16-year-old at the start of my career with Surrey, I remember feeling so sorry for him and it wasn't until years later I realised he didn't give a hoot. For him, what mattered was winning the Test.

The nightwatch

Whereas all the above ninety-niners were either top-class batters or all-rounders who were accomplished batters, Tudes was not selected by England for his batting. He was a high-quality, honest, fast bowler who liked to say he was 'working' on his batting. So when, on the evening of the second day, he was sent in at No. 3 by captain Nasser Hussain as nightwatch, it was a decision tinged as much with hope as expectation. England had been abject in their first innings, falling 100 short of the Kiwis' modest 226, and only Tudes and fellow bowler Andy Caddick managed to top 30. However, the tourists

Nervous Nineties

obligingly collapsed to 107 in their second innings and, despite the questionable pitch, a target of 208 looked gettable. Then, in fading light, England's ever-reliable opener Alec Stewart was immediately bowled for nought – the 31st wicket to fall – leaving his team on 3 for one. Losing another top-order batter at the end of the day was not in Nasser's playbook. He'd already asked his tail-enders for a volunteer nightwatch and 21-year-old Tudor, playing in only his third Test, put up his hand. Just as well because the other main candidates – Phil Tufnell and Alan Mullally – were considered rabbits with the bat. Against fast bowlers and a new ball, neither of them were an attractive option for the skipper.

Personally, I'm not a fan of the nightwatch principle. In the women's game we rarely used it anyway because we mostly played one-dayers. But I could never understand why, at a moment of high tension, you would send out someone who wasn't really a batter in the belief that they could protect the wicket of someone who was. Surely it's a fair bet that you would lose them both. Tudes confirmed my view when he later admitted he hadn't even seen his first ball – a fast yorker from Geoff Allott that missed his off stump by a coat of varnish. Somehow he survived for seven balls before the umpire, Peter Willey, abandoned play due to bad light. The following morning, England were hoping he could simply hang around for a few overs to frustrate the bowlers. It turned out to be more than a few: he added 73 in partnership with Mark Butcher, 98 with Hussain and 37 with Graham Thorpe to secure a seven-wicket win and become the highest-scoring nightwatch in English cricket history, overtaking Harold Larwood's 98 at Melbourne in 1933.

In an interview with Warwickshire's club website years later, Tudor revealed that team manager Graham Gooch had urged him to hit any wide-ish ball pitched in his half of the pitch 'out of the park'. He took the advice, smashing 21 boundaries in an extraordinary three-hour innings. He could hear the crowd chanting his name, willing him on to a maiden century, and when it became obvious that Thorpe was at times denying him the strike in favour of securing the win, they made their displeasure clear. In fact, Thorpe was doing only what his partner had suggested. 'When Thorpey came in, he said: "Look, the game is won, I'll just guide you to your hundred",' recalled Tudes. 'But I said, "Hold on, don't mess around with sport; the wicket's not great, next in is Ramps [Mark Ramprakash], who got zero in the first innings, then its Aftab Habib and Chris Read on their debuts and then the tail. Let's just get the game won." When I got back to the pavilion, I walked in and Tuffers and Butch were fuming at Thorpey and gave him a volley of abuse. I just told them to chill. We'd won a Test match. It's one run. As it turned out, I'm better known for that 99 not out than anything else.'

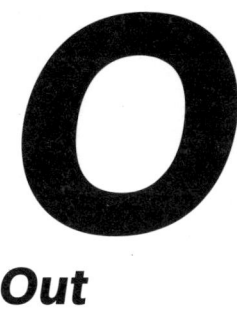

Out

There are officially ten ways of getting out in cricket: bowled, leg before wicket (lbw), caught, run out, obstructing the field, handling the ball, hitting the ball twice, hit wicket, timed out and retired out. However, this being cricket, nothing is straightforward. 'Handling' has now officially been subsumed into 'obstructing the field' even though it is still seen by some traditionalists as a potentially separate breach of the Laws. Life's too short to argue about the merits of combining once-separate methods of dismissal – both of which, incidentally, are incredibly rare – but that won't stop cricket archaists debating it during a rain break. The first three methods of dismissal above, along with hit wicket, are all credited to the bowler. Run-outs are awarded to whichever fielder (including the bowler) throws down the stumps, and the remaining five are the result of a batter getting herself out.

1. Bowled

Surely every bowler's favourite form of dismissal. As a kid you'll play cricket on the street or in the park with no pitch markings, no umpires and precious few rules. But the one rule you do have is that when the ball hits the stumps, and the bails fly off, the batter is out. Once you start playing at higher levels there are irritating caveats – Was it a no-ball? Was the batter ready? Was a fielder distracting her with chat? – but these are comparatively rare. The buzz you get from seeing your ball crash into those timbers never diminishes.

2. Leg before wicket

An lbw gets credited to the bowler on the basis that her crafted delivery has lured the batter into a judgement error. The conditions are that ball pitches in line with stumps, bat misses ball, ball hits pad, and ball would have gone on to hit stumps. At international level, fulfilment of these conditions used to be determined entirely by an umpire with the naked eye, resulting in many a dodgy decision. Club cricketers still have that cross to bear (set aside an hour or two if they want to tell you why they were *never* out) but major international matches now have the benefit of DRS (see H for Howzat), in which ball-tracking technology eliminates any dispute. Two other nuances of lbw are that a batter cannot be out under any circumstances if the ball pitches outside leg stump. She can be out if it pitches outside off stump, but only if she is not playing a shot. There are good reasons for such exemptions; suffice it to say they deter both bowler and batter from employing underhand tactics and, more importantly, make the game more fun to watch.

3. Caught

There are plenty of embarrassing, incompetent things you can do as a fielder, and I've accomplished most of these in my career. Letting a cover drive go straight through your hands for a boundary? Bowlers love you. Failing to back up another fielder shying at the stumps, resulting in four overthrows? Expect your skipper's evil eye. But there's nothing worse than dropping a dolly of a catch. My worst memory of this was fielding in the deep to Katherine Sciver-Brunt's bowling. The batter hit a skier, I was slow to react and then I fumbled the catch. I got an earful of choice language from Katherine, who always believed every ball she bowled should produce a wicket. I thought she'd got it out of her system but, just in case, I slunk into breakfast the following morning, aiming to sit as far away from her as possible. Unfortunately, I dropped my fork as I passed her table. I knew what was coming and, sure enough, Katherine was speaking before the fork had even stopped clattering: 'That's another drop then, Ebz?' I probably deserved it. As a bowler there's nothing worse than bending your back only to have fielders deny you your reward. It happens a lot early in the season, when everyone's hands are freezing. I would carefully set a slip cordon, bowl the perfect away-seamer and find the edge of the bat, only to watch the catch spilt. I would shout down the pitch, asking whether there was 'any danger' of them holding on to one.

In such circumstances the culprit's hope is always that a drop doesn't prove too costly, and that the unnerved batter quickly gets out. But it doesn't necessarily follow. Sometimes the batter will think: *Right, this is clearly my day, time to cash in.* The highest score I ever posted at The Oval was a county match against Wales when I hit 154 not out. I'd been dropped on 6. Every run was a dagger to the heart of the Wales players. In fairness to fielders, they're often unsung heroes whose role rarely gets fully acknowledged in the scorebook. I can bowl a rank long-hop that sits up beautifully to be leathered for six. A boundary fielder might sprint 20 yards, leap balletically to catch the ball mid-air, hang on to it as she crashes painfully onto a rock-hard outfield and get a hug from her team-mates. But it's still my wicket. The scorebook will show it was all me. I do love burgling a wicket.

The concept of 'walking in' as a fielder, which used to be drummed into kids, isn't so applicable to today's game. In white-ball cricket, especially during the Powerplay, fielders stay as close to the edge of the inner ring as they can – not only to intercept potential boundaries but also to snaffle any uppish drives that come their way. The same applies to boundary riders, who know an aerial strike may clear them if they've taken even a couple of steps in from the rope. The simple truth is that batters today are more powerful than ever, thanks to time spent in the gym. And bats are engineered for power-hitting. As a result, players now train to dive and tap back a ball that has flown over the boundary so that a supporting team-mate can still make a catch inside the rope. Provided the tapper-back never has contact with the ground and the ball at the same time, this is perfectly legal. It's why we see these incredible boundary catches in the modern game. Matching players' skill sets to the right fielding position is so important and can be as basic as whether they're left- or right-handed. For example, slips positioned for a right-handed batter shouldn't have a left-handed catcher at the far edge of the cordon because if she has to dive to her right she'll be leading with her 'wrong' hand.

Crowd catches

Crowd catches have become a cherished part of cricket culture. In the Men's 2015 World Cup, staged jointly by Australia and New Zealand, one sponsor promoted a 'catch a million' competition, promising anyone who held a crowd catch the chance of winning $1 million. But there was a snag: the open grass banks that serve as spectator areas at some Kiwi venues became a hunting ground for those committed to the catch-a-million cause. If a six came their way, there would be a stampede towards the landing area, to the detriment of any picnicking families who happened to be in the way. New Zealand Cricket hastily changed the rules, setting up spectator 'catch zones'.

My two favourite crowd-catch chances both occurred in England. The most recent happened at the 2024 Old Trafford Test between England and Sri Lanka as Asitha Fernando bowled a bouncer at Mark Wood. Wood pulled it into the crowd for six, whereupon a male spectator sipping his pint calmly raised his arm to pouch it one-handed. Not a drop of beer was spilt and the England dressing room led the applause. Best of all, though, was Freddie Flintoff's booming six off West Indies pace bowler Jermaine Lawson in the 2004 second Test at Edgbaston. The ball zoomed into the second tier of the Ryder Stand and the hands of one Colin Flintoff, a decent Lancashire League player in his day. Colin couldn't quite hold on, making Freddie the only player ever to have been dropped by his dad during a Test match. 'He's got dreadful hands, has my dad,' the England all-rounder quipped later. 'He plays at weekends and always comes home and tells me what a great catch he's taken. But I think he's proved to everyone today that he's terrible. I thought he was going to fall off the balcony at one stage. He got all excited and put it down.' Flintoff senior was magnanimous in accepting his son's criticism. 'I saw it coming all the way,' he said. 'I should have caught it but in the end I parried the ball straight into Michael Vaughan's mum's lap.' This surely would have counted as a joint parental crowd catch. Sadly, Mrs Vaughan dropped it.

4. Run out

You'd think the Law on scoring a run would be straightforward. Striker and non-striker race to each other's end and ensure some part of their bat or body is grounded behind the popping crease (see G for Ground) before a fielder can break the wicket. The area behind the popping crease is known as the 'batter's ground', whereas the crease itself belongs to the fielders and wicket-keeper. Complexities arise when the wicket is broken at one end while the batters are crossing. In that event the run-out batter is the one nearest the broken wicket or, if they are exactly level, whichever batter was nearer to it immediately prior to their drawing level.

Sometimes a good old-fashioned cock-up occurs when both batters hilariously end up at the same end, usually because one thinks a run can be taken and sets off, while the other thinks 'no chance, pal' and remains steadfastly in her ground. The running batter can't reach safety by joining her partner because that ground is already occupied. Once the wicket is broken at the unoccupied end, she's run out. If you're someone who occasionally struggles to sleep, do keep a copy of 'Law 30: Batter out of his/her ground' by your bedside table. It'll help you nod off in no time.

The Laws of Cricket must of course be written precisely enough to cope with any possible scenario. But that's easier said than done – as the 'bouncing bat' controversy, which saw two England players dismissed in matches 14 months apart, demonstrated. The first occurred in January 2014 during a T20I at the Melbourne Cricket Ground. Eoin Morgan pushed for a single and appeared to make it – despite Australia's Brad Hodge brilliantly throwing down the stumps from cover. However, the momentum of Morgan's dive had caused his bat to bounce up so that no part of it, or him, was in contact with the ground in the instant the wicket was broken. Then, in March 2015, precisely the same fate befell Chris Jordan as he aborted a run attempt during England's ill-fated World Cup campaign. Bangladesh all-rounder Shakib Al Hasan threw down the stumps a split second after the diving Jordan had made his ground. But, again, a bouncing bat meant he was in mid-air as the bails came off. Simon Fry was on duty as third umpire for both matches and correctly concluded from TV replays that in each case the batter was out. This resulted in a long-overdue review of Law 30 and in 2017 the custodians of the Laws, Marylebone Cricket Club (see One Game . . . But Which Format?), decided that the existing wording was neither fair nor logical and changed it as follows: '30.1.2 However, a batter shall not be considered to be out of his/her ground if, in running or diving towards his/her ground and beyond, and having grounded some part of his/her person or bat beyond the popping crease, there is subsequent loss of contact between the ground and any part of his/her person or bat, or between the bat and person.' Glad we've cleared that up.

Notwithstanding the above, run-outs usually fall into two categories: either a batter misjudges the danger of taking a run (see Allan Donald in Q for Quick Singles) or they think the risk is acceptable, only to be outdone by a fielder's direct hit on the stumps (see Nathan Lyon in F for Form). Yet there is a third category – the 'Mankad' – and here's where the fun really starts.

The Mankad

The Mankad is a legitimate run-out dismissal in cricket but you'll have wars in changing rooms and commentary boxes over its use. It happens when the batter at the non-striker's end moves out of her crease to try and sneak a quick single – known as 'backing up' – just as the bowler is delivering the ball. A bowler who spots this can stop before she reaches the high point of her delivery action, turn and whip off the bails. Under Law 38.3, this counts as a run-out.

Before we go any further, we should look at the incident that christened the Mankad along with its eponymous exponent. In November 1947, 17 Indian cricketers travelled to Australia – the first to represent their newly independent country on the international stage. Among them was Mulvantrai Himmatlal Mankad – better known as Vinoo – a 30-year-old opening batter and left-arm spinner considered one of the best all-rounders of his day. He would need every weapon in his armoury if India were to compete against an Australian team who would later be dubbed 'Don Bradman's Invincibles'. By the time they arrived at the Sydney Cricket Ground for the second Test, the tourists were already 1–0 down.

In an earlier warm-up game, Mankad had warned the great Aussie opening bat Bill Brown against trying to pinch a run by backing up. Now he saw Brown was at it again, moving a yard outside the non-striker's batting crease before he delivered the ball. This time there was no warning. Mankad paused in his delivery stride, whipped off the bails and the furious Brown was out – face like thunder as the Indians celebrated wildly. Elements of the Australian press were less enamoured, whinging on about the demise of sportsmanship and the so-called spirit of cricket. Yet not everyone agreed. Under the headline 'Shocking Display', the wonderfully titled *Melbourne Truth* wrote: 'Brown might feel aggrieved at Mankad's action but nobody would support him. Brown's continuing offence in this matter is so blatant that he will have to give serious consideration to it if he desires to retain his position in the Australian XI.' Over in Adelaide, *The Advertiser* quoted Aussie selector Hugh Bridgman asking: 'What if a batsman scrapes home by three inches after cribbing a yard at the start? Isn't that taking an unfair advantage?' Even Brown's captain, the great Bradman himself, defended Mankad: 'For the life of me,' he wrote later in his autobiography, 'I cannot understand why [the press] questioned his sportsmanship. The laws of cricket make it quite clear that the non-striker must keep within his ground until the ball has been delivered. If not, why is the provision there which enables the bowler to run him out?' I'm with Bradman here. As a bowler I'd always warn batters if I saw them trying to pinch a single off me – although I never actually Mankaded anyone, for reasons I explain below.

Mankads in any form of cricket are rare, although in recent years there have been some notable incidents in the women's one-day format. Perhaps the most ruthless enforcer of the rule was Cameroon's Maeva Douma who, during an ICC T20 World Cup Africa Group B qualifier at Gaborone in 2021, Mankaded four of her opponents. They included three of the top four batters – Kevin Awino, Rita Musamali and captain Immaculate Nakisuuyi – along with the No. 6, Janet Mbabazi. You can perhaps see why Douma was taking no prisoners. She must have known her side's batting line-up was flaky and, sure enough, in response to Uganda's 190 for six, Cameroon posted just 35. The main thing that comes to mind, however, when you reflect on this game is: where on earth was Uganda's coach? Once the first two batters had been Mankaded, someone in the management team should have been hopping up and down, throwing teacups. If you're up against a bowler this committed, don't blithely carry on sneaking out of your ground – wait for the ball to be bowled. After Douma Mankaded two more Ugandans she probably thought she was on for a Mankad five-fer (five wickets credited to the bowler) but sadly it was not to be.

This was one of those occasions where a glance at the scorebook wouldn't tell the whole story. It would show only that Douma had run out four batters – not *how* she'd run them out. That said, four Mankads would surely convince a conscientious scorer to write some explanatory note in the margin. Douma was savage in her application of Law 38.3, but ultimately the batting side must take responsibility. She followed the rules; her opponents didn't. The Mankad is clearly embraced in Cameroonian women's cricket because in May 2024 bowler Olive Ranedoumoun used it to dismiss Rwanda opener Marie Bimenyimana for one during the Kwibuka Women's T20 tournament in Kigali. That didn't help Cameroon much either: chasing Rwanda's 141, they succumbed for 39.

In the women's game the most high-profile Mankad dismissal of recent years came at the home of cricket in September 2022, as India and England fought out a tense finale to their third ODI at Lord's. India had batted first, racking up 169, with all-rounder Deepti Sharma top-scoring on 68 not out. In reply England seemed doomed to a third successive defeat, falling to 53 for six in the 15th over. But a lower-order fightback somehow kept them in contention and, by the start of the 44th over, a last-wicket partnership between Charlie Dean and Freya Davies had left them just 16 runs short of an unlikely victory. Then off-spinner Deepti Sharma noticed Dean backing up too far at the non-striker's end, whipped off the bails and delivered India their series whitewash.

Why warn?

In my era the Mankad was not the done thing. You wouldn't have been popular with your own coaches and team-mates, never mind your opponents. Although there would be lots of warnings and cheeky smiles, I never saw it happen in a game because everyone obeyed the unwritten rule. I never understood why. Why should there be a warning? Footballers don't warn of a quick free kick; tennis players don't give notice of a crafty drop shot. You're not there to help opponents. My strong view was – and is – that the non-striker should stay within her crease until the ball is released. That's the *actual* rule. If you ignore it trying to gain an advantage then good luck, especially if there's a spinner on, but don't complain if you get run out. We had a big debate in the commentary box about this after Charlie Dean's dismissal but I still believe Mankads should be acceptable both to the spirit and the letter of the law. And, frankly, I find them fun.

5. Obstructing the field

Obstructing the field is a type of dismissal under Law 37 in which a batter 'wilfully attempts to obstruct or distract the fielding side by word or action'. It now includes 'handling the ball', although (as mentioned above) this is still considered a separate form of dismissal by scorebook traditionalists. They will defiantly point out that books completed before 2016 will record 'handling the ball' as a method of getting out and, therefore, the term should not be airbrushed out of the cricket lexicon. I'm going along with that in this list, mainly to justify retelling one notable and controversial incident in which a Test batter was given out for picking up the ball and helpfully handing it to an opponent. (More on that later.) Obstructing the field is incredibly rare – at the time of writing, there have been fewer than two dozen international instances recorded. It is aimed at punishing batters who have stopped a fielder from catching, retrieving or throwing the ball or who have deliberately used their bat or body to prevent a throw hitting the stumps. The latter scenario was pivotal in two of those 17 dismissals – both involving England batters: my former Surrey colleague Jason Roy and England captain Ben Stokes.

Jason's obstruction offence occurred during a T20 game against South Africa in June 2017. It needs to be set in the context of how you're permitted to run between the wickets – namely, that you must maintain your 'running line'. You can't sprint down the middle of the pitch – umpires go apoplectic if they see that because of the potential damage caused by your boots – so you take one side and stick to it. It's normally obvious. The bowler chooses which side of the stumps to deliver the ball, and the non-striker stands the other side. If the batters go for a run, the striker takes a running line along the opposite side of the pitch to his partner. It's worth saying here that either batter can call for a run, and that's the cause of many a hilarious cock-up (see the Allan Donald run-out in Q for Quick Singles). The call should ideally come from whichever player is running to the 'danger end' – typically the stumps closest to the fielder retrieving the ball. Jason's mistake was to change the side he was running as he scrambled back to his crease after backing up (see Mankads, above). This resulted in the fielder's return throw hitting him when it could conceivably have hit the stumps. South Africa appealed, and the third umpire decided that Jason had deliberately changed course and was therefore out obstructing the field. The crowd booed, although there was no reason to; it is irrelevant whether the ball would have hit the stumps and, for me, the Law was correctly interpreted.

Ben's dismissal in September 2015 was arguably more controversial because his 'obstruction' was a split-second natural reaction to seeing a ball thrown towards his head. Natural it may have been, but it was also deliberate. He was batting in an ODI run chase when he hit a bump-ball (where the batter drives the ball down into the pitch, causing it to 'bump' into the air) straight back to Australian bowler Mitchell Starc. Starc caught it one-handed and, seeing Stokes had set off for a run, shied at the stumps. In response, Stokes ducked and raised his hand to palm the ball away while diving back into his ground. Starc appealed, Aussie captain Steve Smith declined the captain's prerogative to withdraw it (another convention of etiquette) and the third umpire decided Stokes was out.

The only England Test batter to have been given out obstructing the field was the greatest of them all, Sir Len Hutton. In 1951, during the fifth Test against South Africa at The Oval, a ball from Athol Rowan spun sharply, struck his glove, which the Laws consider to be an extension of the bat, and ballooned behind to where wicket-keeper Russell Endean was waiting. Hutton twisted round to try and bat it away but missed and the ball bounced harmlessly clear of the stumps. Because his wild swing had prevented Endean from attempting the catch – it could easily have taken a few teeth out – Hutton became the first Test player to be out obstructing the field. Curiously, had he made contact with the ball, the scorebook would instead have recorded 'out hitting the ball twice' (see below).

6. Handled the ball

In one of those mouthwatering twists of fate – sit up at the back, sports trivia fans – Russell Endean was himself out in similar circumstances during another South Africa–England encounter. Playing in the second innings of the second Test at Newlands Cricket Ground, Cape Town, in 1957, he edged a ball that then bobbed up over his stumps. Instinctively Endean turned and used his free hand to swat it away. This was a contravention of what was then Law 33 – stating that once a batter had hit the ball he could only legally 'guard' his wicket (i.e. prevent the ball from going on to hit the stumps) by using his bat, a hand holding the bat or any part of his body other than a free hand. Had Endean deflected the ball with a flying kung fu kick, he'd have been fine – provided he didn't stop England keeper Godfrey Evans (see K for Keepers) going for the catch.

Two England players have been given out handled the ball during Test matches. The first was Graham Gooch in 1993 during the first Ashes Test at Old Trafford. Facing Aussie paceman Merv Hughes on 133, he failed to control a ball that popped up before he turned to flick it away with the back of his hand. Gooch was bang to rights; however, the second England captain to be dismissed for handling, Michael Vaughan, can count himself unfortunate. Playing in the third Test at Bengaluru, he was well set on 64 when he missed his attempted sweep to India spinner Sarandeep Singh. The ball looped up as he stayed in his kneeling position before it landed on his trousers and fell to the floor. At that point, Vaughan grabbed it and threw it to the nearby short-leg fielder. TV commentators at the time were divided on the dismissal. Some argued that Vaughan was trying to be helpful by returning the ball to the fielding side. Others suggested he may have been fearful that the ball could spin back onto his stumps and reacted a little too quickly.

But neither Englishman's handling dismissal remotely compares to that of Andrew Hilditch during a bad-tempered series between Australia and Pakistan in March 1979. Playing in the second Test at the WACA in Perth, Hilditch was on 87 at the non-striker's end when he picked up a stationary ball from a wayward throw and passed it back to the bowler, Sarfraz Nawaz. Sarfraz immediately appealed and Hilditch had to go.

7. Hitting the ball twice

This seems so unlikely, but the idea always made me nervous. If you block a ball and tap it back to the bowler as a courtesy, you can theoretically be out hitting the ball twice – even if it's obvious you had no intention of taking a run. I recall a few occasions when a fielding side tried such an appeal – none were upheld – and in fact, the only incident ever recorded in the modern professional game occurred at Romania's Moara Vlasiei Cricket Ground during a Continental Cup T20I group qualifier between Romania and Malta on 20 August 2023. Malta's wicket-keeper Fanyan Mughal took a wild mow at a delivery from Shantanu Vashisht. He missed and the ball bounced off his arm, landing a few feet in front of him. Mughal looked up, suddenly aware (a) that his batting partner Gopal Thakur had come charging down the pitch and (b) that Romania wicket-keeper Satvik Nadigotla was about to pounce and try to run Thakur out at the non-striker's end. In response, Mughal tapped the ball down the wicket, out of Nadigotla's reach, and was instantly given out hitting the ball twice. His action would have been legal only if, in the opinion of the umpire, he'd been trying to guard his wicket from the dropping ball. This hitting the ball twice Law is thought to have been introduced sometime in the mid-seventeenth century as a safety precaution, preventing batters from pushing the ball a few yards, charging after it and giving it a second clout. The safety factor arose because fielders would also be charging after it and so on occasions also got clouted.

8. Hit wicket

This is a surprisingly common way to get out in both the men's and women's game, with more than 300 examples on record across all three professional formats. Under Law 35 the striker is out 'hit wicket' if her bat, part of her bat (i.e. a splinter), or any part of her 'person' (including protective gear) breaks the wicket with the ball in play. Put simply, it's all over for a batter who knocks off the bails while receiving the ball or setting off for a run. The most noteworthy example in English cricket occurred in August 1991 during the fifth Test against West Indies at The Oval. In trying to hook Curtly Ambrose, Ian Botham lost balance and fell over his stumps. The dismissal caused uproar in the *Test Match Special* commentary box later as Brian Johnston observed that Botham 'just didn't quite get his leg over'. This double entendre provoked a giggling meltdown between Johnston and co-presenter Jonathan Agnew – an exchange that BBC Radio 5 Live listeners later voted as the greatest sporting commentary of all time.

Hit wickets caused by splintering bats tend to belong to a bygone age. In the 1921 Ashes Test at Headingley, England's Andy Ducat edged a quick delivery from Ted McDonald, causing a splinter to break off and dislodge a bail. The ball continued to the slip cordon, where it was safely pouched and, although the hit wicket offence occurred first, Ducat was given out caught. In the modern game, falling head gear has become the more likely cause of this form of dismissal, most memorably when a quick bouncer from West Indies' Dwayne Bravo cannoned into England's Kevin Pietersen's helmet during the third Test at Old Trafford in 2007. So great was the force that it broke the Velcro fastening on Pietersen's chin strap, sending his helmet flying onto the stumps.

9. Timed out

Another rarity. An incoming batter gets three minutes after a wicket falls to be ready and standing at the crease. I cannot understand why this might be challenging – personally, I could never wait to get out there – although perhaps, if a cluster of wickets fell very quickly, a lower-order batter might be in the loo or struggling to locate a piece of kit. The only two incidents of a timed out dismissal in international cricket both occurred in 2023. The first involved Sri Lanka's iconic all-rounder Angelo Mathews during an ICC Men's World Cup ODI group-stage match against Bangladesh in Delhi. Mathews had got to the wicket but as he tightened his chin strap it broke and he decided to call for a new helmet. He showed Bangladesh captain Shakib Al Hasan the problem, but Shakib refused to withdraw his appeal and Mathews was given out. He returned to the dressing room, throwing equipment in his wake. Bangladesh then chased down Sri Lanka's 279, leaving Mathews the one consolation of claiming Shakib's wicket.

The aftermath of this match caused much bitterness in the Sri Lankan camp, with Mathews querying 'where the common sense went'. For his part, Shakib pointed out that he was only following the Laws. 'I feel like I was at a war,' he said, 'so I had to take a decision to make sure my team wins.' The situation was complicated because, although the Laws allow a maximum of three minutes for incoming batters to be ready, the time limit can be adjusted according to tournament rules. In the case of the ICC Men's World Cup, it was reduced to two minutes. 'The TV umpire monitors the two minutes and he will then relay the message to the standing umpire,' explained fourth umpire Adrian Holdstock. 'The batter wasn't ready within those two minutes even before the strap became an issue for him . . . as a batter you need to make sure all your equipment is in place.' Six weeks later Ghana's Godfred Bakiweyem became the first cricketer to be timed out in a T20I when he failed to get his act together during a Group B Africa Cricket Association Cup match in Benoni, South Africa. But at least Godfred was in the ground; in 2002, when former West Indian Test player Vasbert Drakes was timed out during a Border v Free State first-class match in East London, South Africa, it was because his inbound plane from the Caribbean was still flying.

10. Retired out

This is where you are asked to give yourself out so that your team-mates can have a go. It's not the same as 'retired hurt', where the batter would have carried on if she could. In pre-season club and county warm-up games we all got retired out and you accept that everyone needs a bit of practice time in the middle. I didn't like it; if I'm scoring runs, let me carry on. But if the skipper waves you in, it's not a good idea to argue. In international cricket the first player to be retired out was

Out

Marvan Atapattu, playing for Sri Lanka against Bangladesh in the 2001 Asian Test Championships. Bangladesh are a good side these days but back then they had only just arrived on the international stage and were abject. They were bundled out for 90 in 36.4 overs, with Muttiah Muralitharan taking five wickets for 13 runs inside ten overs. Talk about entering the lion's den. Sri Lanka ended day one on 246 for one and were 436 for two at lunch on day two. Soon after, Atapattu completed his fifth double hundred in Test cricket and his captain, Sanath Jayasuriya, waved him back to the pavilion. That wasn't even the end of the humiliation: Mahela Jayawardene also got retired out after posting 150. Chasing a mammoth 555, Bangladesh at least recovered some pride with a second-innings total of 328. They lost by an innings and 137 runs.

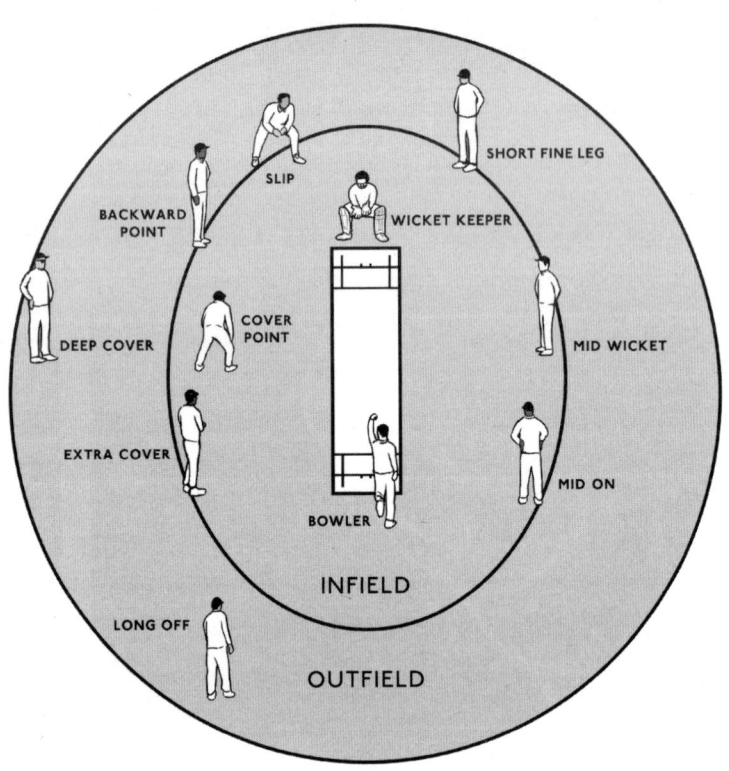

Powerplay

Powerplay is a feature of limited-overs cricket. It deters the fielding side from pursuing negative tactics while encouraging batters to hit big. By imposing restrictions on the number of boundary fielders at crucial stages of an innings, it increases the intensity of a match and prompts captains to seek innovative strategies. Crowds love it, although many bowlers argue that Powerplay has tipped the balance of play too far in favour of the batter. While that may be true, it's the same for both sides.

Here's how it works. A fielding 'circle' – actually an oval – is drawn on the outfield by marking two semi-circles, the boundaries of which extend 30 yards from middle stump at either end. This indicates an 'infield' and an 'outfield'. In a T20 match, only two fielders are allowed to stand in the outfield during the first six overs; this increases to a maximum of five fielders for the remainder of the innings. In ODIs the rules are slightly different: Powerplay One covers the first ten overs and, again, only two fielders are permitted outside the inner circle; Powerplay Two, from the 11th to the 40th over, permits up to four fielders outside the circle; Powerplay Three, the final ten overs, increases the maximum to five. In

The Hundred, Powerplay restrictions are active only for the first quarter of the game – 25 legal balls – and also limit outfield patrollers to two.

There's always a feelgood factor to claiming a wicket early in the first Powerplay because this will probably be a high-value Fast Starter (see B for Batting). Straight away, you've forced your opponents into rethinking their strategy. But posting dot balls is also important: you want to put batters under pressure from the get-go, and if they haven't scored for a few balls it might push them into attempting a reckless shot. Quick bowlers will look to bang the ball in on a good length, making it difficult to cut or drive. They'll want to beat the batter for pace and induce snicks behind, so that may mean starting with a couple of slip catchers and setting a third man or fine leg to avoid conceding boundaries off the bat edge. However, battle plans rarely survive contact with the enemy. If opening batters get off to a flyer, or the surface isn't conducive to pace or movement, a skipper will quickly move to preplanned variations such as protecting one side of the outfield. To use Moeen Ali as an example, he spins the ball into the right-hander and bowls tight to the body, so that means packing his leg-side field – the area the batter is most likely to target. In the modern game there's an argument for hitting *against* the spin, but not all players are comfortable with that. Whatever, the general principle to protect one side holds good; it allows you to probe a line and length and forces the batter to take bigger risks.

In the above Moeen scenario, batters will consider counter-measures such as stepping to leg and hitting through the off side (England's Harry Brook is adept at this) or performing a reverse sweep to find off-side gaps. There will also be a case for charging down the wicket to straight-drive

Moeen in the hope of unsettling his length. It is all a cat-and-mouse affair. Moeen could 'dangle the carrot' by leaving a temptingly large gap on the leg side while bowling wide of off stump. Depending on the stage of the game, the batter might go for that gap, but it's a high-risk shot against a class international bowler. These personal duels are what make the game so compelling.

Fill your boots

For the batting side it's vital during early Powerplay overs to fill their boots with runs. With gaping spaces around the boundary, any well-timed shot punched through or over the infield circle is likely to bring fours or sixes. For me, as an opening batter, it felt almost designed for my natural game. Seam bowlers would come on and I could get great value for my shots. I didn't need to bother about changing my technique. But as time went on, and Powerplay tactics evolved, spinners got into the action much earlier. And England were facing the best in the world: players like Shelley Nitschke and Lisa Sthalekar of Australia, India's Gouher Sultana and Pakistan's Sana Mir. My only attacking shot against them was to charge down the wicket, get to the pitch of the ball and smack it before it spun. Don't get me wrong, I loved nothing better than charging a bowler, but opposing spinners knew this too. They worked out my game plan and bowled a wider line. I'd end up miles outside my crease, missing my shot and getting stumped. The coaches decided I needed to add options to my game, so I was given the choice between working on the traditional, flat, sweep shot to leg, the slog sweep or – and this was the new kid on the block – the reverse sweep to off. I was bad at all of them, partly because of my persistent back injury but also because it felt like such an unnatural movement.

Between 2008 and 2012 I was sent off to various camps in India and worked with a specialist coach there. It was amazing. In England, you'd have a two-hour session and be done. In India, you'd be up at 6am and it would be breakfast, nets, lunch, nets, dinner, nets and finally bed. You'd be practising shots 14 hours a day, in the baking heat, with a few drinks breaks thrown in. Around 20 fantastic young spinners would arrive from nowhere and queue up to bowl at you. Indian spinners, I discovered, absolutely love bowling. My coach, Umesh Patel, would rough up the ground or put down mats to enhance the movement of balls that were already fizzing at you. They'd use golf balls or extra bouncy balls. They'd hand you a specially adapted thin bat in case you found the set-up too easy. Fat chance. I never really mastered the reverse sweep but I was learning it late in my career – in my late twenties – whereas today's young cricketers play it from the age of about ten. At least by the time I left India I understood my options. Which came down to making fast decisions about playing forward or back, or slog sweeping. It was hard to adjust because I didn't *want* to adjust but, against bowlers who had worked out my game, there was no choice.

Finally, there's the role of fielders during Powerplays. Within the circle, they should be on their toes for run-out chances and the prevention of quick or easy singles. They must certainly avoid the unforgivable howler of straying outside the circle once posted because, if a team exceeds the permitted number of outfielders at the point the bowler delivers, the umpire will call no-ball and award the on-strike player a free hit. This is effectively a risk-free slog because the batter becomes temporarily immune to being bowled, caught or out lbw. As for specialist boundary-riders, they'll need to have mastered both the dive-stop and the 'flying tap-back', where they try and pat a ball zooming over the boundary back to a team-mate waiting inside the rope to catch it. This is a perfectly legal catch so long as (a) the tapper-back's first contact with the ball is inside the boundary and (b) the tapper-back hasn't touched both ball and ground behind the boundary at the same time. The tap-back technique – a fielding drill developed to counter increased boundary-hitting in limited-overs matches – has emerged only relatively recently but has quickly become one of the most thrilling spectacles in cricket.

Q
Quick Singles

I got roasted by coaches when I moved up to international cricket because I liked to stand and admire my shots. They would call me over for a conversation that always began: 'Ebony, why are you missing so many runs?' It was hard to give a credible answer. I was left in no doubt that as you advanced up the levels in cricket, small margins mattered much more and every run was potentially match-winning. I had to learn to back up, to be on my toes when called for a single. I had to practise calling runs off my own shots, assessing the time I had to make my ground as well as the run-out risk to my partner. Starting out, I found some of the calls baffling. What did my batting partner mean by 'wait on'? Wait on what? It was confusing terminology that everyone just assumed you understood. My one get-out-of-jail card was that I could run fast. Although I could be slow to react to a poached single, or the need to get back inside my crease, when I did react I moved pretty darn quick.

Clarity is the most important thing when it comes to running singles and, while that might sound obvious to club cricketers, it's easy to forget that the international game is played at greater pace. Decisions are required in microseconds and in high-pressure moments they inevitably go wrong. The most excruciating example came during the semi-final of the 1999 World Cup at Edgbaston – still seen by fans and pundits alike as one of the greatest games in ODI history. South Africa had dismissed Australia for a modest 213 and were freewheeling to victory on 48 for none when Shane Warne produced one of his devastating cameos to reduce them to 61 for four. A half-century from Jacques Kallis, and vital middle-order runs from Jonty Rhodes and Shaun Pollock kept the Proteas in the game, but as the overs ticked down and the wickets tumbled it seemed they had blown it. Then all-rounder Lance Klusener cut loose, bludgeoning 31 off 15 balls to tie the scores with three balls to spare. On the face of it, any captain would have taken that scenario at the start. Klusener on strike against the bowling of Damien Fleming, with three chances to hit one run and secure a place in the World Cup final? No problem. But there were snags.

Firstly, if a wicket fell, a tie was no good to South Africa. Australia would go through thanks to a better net run rate in the Super Six round. Secondly, South Africa's last man, Allan Donald, was at the non-striker's end and, while Donald was a great fast bowler, he was a rabbit with the bat. Even so, Proteas fans reassured themselves that everything was OK: Klusener was facing so Donald's services wouldn't be required. Meanwhile, with no other cards left to play, Aussie skipper Steve Waugh brought his entire field inside the circle in the hope of stopping the crucial single. He would also have noted how Donald, still on nought and looking anxious and nervy, had ventured far out of his crease on the third ball of Fleming's over to try and nab it. Had Darren Lehmann's throw from mid-on hit the stumps, Donald would have been run out and Australia would be in the final. But Lehmann missed.

Cue the next scene of this outrageous sporting drama. Fleming's fourth delivery was mishit by Klusener straight to Mark Waugh at mid-off and Klusener set off, barrelling down the pitch for a risky winning run. Had Donald responded immediately, he might just have made it. But he was watching the ball and, amid deafening crowd noise, didn't hear Klusener's call. He stuttered to the middle of the wicket, froze wide-eyed, dropped his bat, was gleefully run out by wicket-keeper Adam Gilchrist, and sent Australia to a final in which they easily beat Pakistan.

Every tail-ender in the world must have felt empathy with Donald in his moment of anguish. That said, a panicky mix-up under huge pressure at the denouement of an extraordinary game is not the worst batting crime in cricket. That label is reserved for batters who go for a quick single – and would have *completed* a quick single – if only they had stretched or dived and grounded their bat into the crease. Failing to ground your bat is what you might call 'very village', a reference to adult club cricketers who commit a schoolkid howler. When you walk back into a changing room after being run out like that, you can expect cold stares and rolling eyes from your team-mates. Diving is a high-level skill in cricket, practised regularly in the professional game, and full-stretch dives that put your body on the line in tight margin calls is an expectation not an individual choice. Batters have to learn how to dive for the crease. Get it wrong and you can end up jamming the bat into the pitch instead of sliding it in. The impact could mean you lose your grip of the bat – and therefore get run out despite your dive – or sustain a jarring injury.

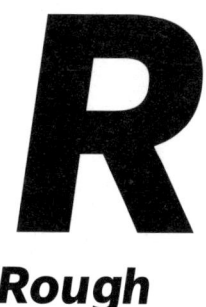

Rough

Roughing up the pitch (so that a spinning or seaming ball 'bites' better) or the ball itself (so that it moves more through the air) have long been the murkiest of cricket's dark arts. The only fair way for a team to adapt a pitch to their best interests is by asking the ground staff in advance to prepare a faster or slower surface, perhaps one devoid of grass for their batters or showing the odd green patch to encourage the bowlers. Use of heavy or light rollers during a game can legally affect how quickly a surface deteriorates, but sometimes the pitch gets a little 'help' to deteriorate. I certainly played in sides that would try to provide that help. Umpires would be on the lookout for fielders walking on the wicket, and you'd get lambasted if you were spotted. So fielders crossing from one side of the outfield to the other between overs would make a big show of jumping over it to get into the umpire's head that the surface was being respected. As time in the game wore on, they'd start dragging their trailing boot on a length so that the studs roughened the surface, making it easier for a ball to grip and spin. My own attempts at this were largely hopeless. The studs on my trailing boot once caught in the ground, resulting in a full-on belly flop. It was hard to pretend I'd tripped over one of the flattest pieces of turf in the country.

When it comes to roughening or polishing the ball's surface, the rules are tight. Law 41.3.2 says fielders are allowed to polish, clean or dry it but anything else amounts to unfair play. When the ball is new, the aim is to shine one side of the seam using sweat and a good trouser-rub while allowing the other to roughen – desirable conditions for the ball to swing (see S for Seam, Swing and Spin). A roughened ball is also easier for the spinners to grip (see C for Coloured Balls). You can try advancing the roughening process by firing the ball into the wicket-keeper so that it bounces two or three times on the rough side before she takes it. If we wanted to scuff a specific side of the seam, which is quite difficult, I would hold the stitching horizontally and skim the ball into the keeper with the target side at the bottom. These days umpires are much tougher on this practice. If they spot it happening too often, they're liable to stride over and threaten five penalty runs against your team.

Aussie ball-tampering

In the past, ball-tampering tricks have included makeshift polishes such as hair wax, lip salve, suntan lotion, Vaseline – even saliva after sucking a sweet. Scuffing aids have involved everything from bottle tops and pocket zips to sandpaper and boot studs. But in recent years, with TV cameras covering every corner of the ground, all this has become a risky business. In 2018 Australia found themselves at the centre of Sandpapergate, the most blatant cheating scandal of the modern era. Their Test series against South Africa was level at 1–1 but by the afternoon of 24 March – the third day of the third Test in Cape Town – the hosts had seized the momentum. Now in their second innings, they were cruising towards a 200-run lead with plenty of batting to come. The tourists needed wickets and fast. Shortly after lunch, TV cameras zoned in on Cameron Bancroft, a relative newcomer to the Australian squad, who appeared to be rubbing the ball with a yellow object. Surprisingly, he was rubbing the rough side of the ball – the opposite side to that he would have been expected to shine on his trousers. But he wasn't interested in shining; severely roughening one side would increase the possibility of reverse swing and with world-class quick bowlers like Pat Cummins, Mitchell Starc and Josh Hazlewood in the team, this could be a match-winner.

Embarrassingly for Bancroft, his actions were seen not only by millions of TV viewers but also on screens around the ground. Moments later, Aussie substitute fielder Peter Handscomb came onto the outfield and exchanged words with Bancroft, prompting him to put something down the front of his trousers. The whole scene felt like a Whitehall farce. When the umpires approached, Bancroft produced a sunglasses pouch from his pocket and his explanation was accepted. No penalty runs were awarded and the ball continued in play. But by the end-of-day press conference everything was unravelling. Bancroft first claimed the yellow object was abrasive tape that had picked up sand and grit. That didn't make his behaviour OK but at least he could argue it was unplanned. The line held for only five days. Cricket Australia's investigation revealed the 'tape' was sandpaper and that the ball-roughing plan had been hatched by a 'leadership group' including captain Steve Smith and vice-captain David Warner. Both were suspended for 12 months while Bancroft, the junior party, got a nine-month ban. It must be said that ball-tampering is by no means the preserve of the Aussies. Over the past 30 years some of cricket's biggest names have been disciplined, including Shoaib Akhtar (Pakistan), Waqar Younis (Pakistan), Vernon Philander (South Africa), Faf du Plessis (South Africa), Rahul Dravid (India) and Michael Atherton (England).

Illegal ball-roughening has now been largely drummed out of international cricket and, as a result, teams have changed tack. Now if a ball is seen as 'unhelpful', the fielding captain will try to get it changed, claiming it has become misshapen. This is where you'll see umpires produce a gauge – it looks for all the world like a pair of handcuffs – to check. If a ball has been knocked out of shape, they will call for a box of older balls and try to find a replacement in similar condition. Seeking a ball change, even if the umpires refuse it, can work as a sneaky tactic to try and unsettle a batter who is well set. She'll want to get on with things; the last thing she'll need is a break in play while her opponents discuss the finer points of geometry with the umpire.

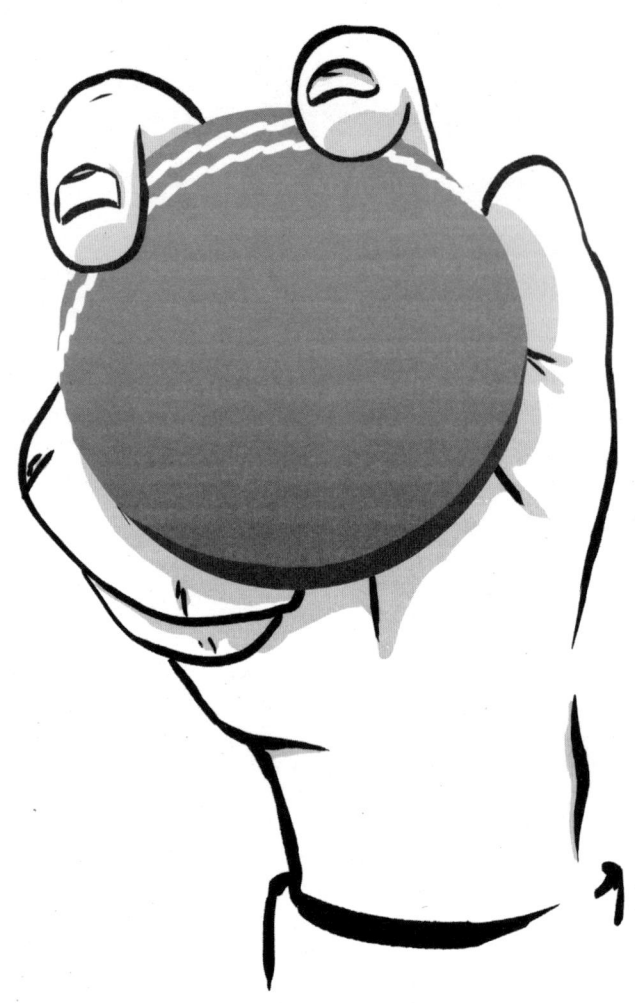

S

Seam, Swing and Spin

For a bowler, seeing your ball demolish the wickets is pure euphoria. My dream delivery either shapes away from the right-hander, misses the bat edge and takes the top of off stump or it nips back and goes between bat and pad to hit middle. You train so hard to see this happen. Hundreds of balls in the nets, honing line and length, working on accuracy and yet, even when you produce that beautiful ball, the batter can still get lucky and edge it through the slips for four. It doesn't feel fair. Toiling away for no reward. And then suddenly it all comes together. Sometimes you know the second it leaves your hand – *this is the one* – and then boom, the bails are flying, your team-mates are jumping, the batter's staring back in disbelief. An lbw is nice, a catch in the slips – lovely. But there's nothing like a ball that rearranges the stumps. While this book isn't a coaching manual, it's worth briefly setting out the characteristics of the three main ball brands and what different types of bowlers are trying to do with them (see also C for Coloured Balls and R for Rough).

The weight and size of balls is specified under the Laws. For men this is between 5.5 and 5.75 oz, with a circumference of between 8.81 and 9 in., and for women between 4.94

and 5.31 oz and a circumference of between 8.25 and 8.88 in. Balls are made in similar ways: a central core of cork covered by tightly wound strings, with four pieces of leather sewn together as the covering. But within these parameters, the designs adopted by manufacturers make a significant difference to the outcome of Test matches. For a start, the brand used in international cricket depends on where the match is being played. Kookaburra is the usual go-to in Australia, New Zealand, South Africa, Pakistan and Bangladesh. Dukes is favoured in England, the West Indies and Ireland, while India's home Tests are played with an SG ball. All three are high-quality products but are subtly different. This affects the way they perform.

The Kookaburra has a flatter seam and tends to seam and swing more (see below) in the early overs of an innings. It is also considered easier to grip by spin bowlers. But it softens earlier and the surface scuffs faster due to fewer coats of lacquer. This is good news for batters if they can survive the first 15–20 overs of an innings because the Kookaburra's bounce and movement then becomes more predictable. Unfortunately for seam bowlers, predictability is a curse. That's why roughing up one side of the ball to create the potential for greater swing – a process not always done legally (see R for Rough) – is such a temptation for fielding sides.

Whereas the Kookaburra is partly machine-sewn, the Dukes is completely hand-stitched, resulting in a more prominent seam. It has an extra coat of lacquer, which helps repel moisture common in English conditions, and because the shine lasts longer the ball will – depending on the weather and pitch – swing and seam around deep into an innings, which is perfect for England's quicker bowlers. The SG ball has similar hand-stitching and durability, while its pronounced, wide seam offers sharp turn and bounce for spinners – particularly helpful to India's pantheon of spinners bowling on abrasive Indian wickets.

Seam bowling

I was able to seam the ball both ways off the pitch, but my stock delivery as a side-on bowler (see A for Actions) would bounce away from the right-handed batter. Later in my career I became more chest-on, producing deliveries that moved into the right-hander. Whatever the action, the basic aim for all quicks and medium-pacers is to bowl 'seam up', in other words with the seam vertical so that when the ball bounces it can hopefully bite into the pitch and divert slightly. If there are any cracks or rough patches in front of the batter then the seamer may try to pitch onto them to heighten the effect. A seam-up grip usually has the index and middle finger either side of the stitching with the ball resting on the third finger. Variations include tilting the angle of the seam or even holding two fingers directly across it, a grip known as 'wobble seam'.

Swing bowling

Swing and seam bowling are not mutually exclusive and if you can produce the odd ball that does both then you're a truly formidable prospect for batters. A new ball is lacquered, so if you can keep shining one side only, the physics of flight will ensure that the rougher side creates increased disturbance in the air around it. This results in a swerve in direction, or what cricketers call 'swing'. The direction of swing depends on whether the shiny side is positioned to the left or right of the seam (a useful indicator to the watching batter), while the seam itself acts as a rudder. If the shiny side is on the right of a right-handed bowler's grip, the ball is set to swing away. If it is on the left the ball is positioned to swing in. Once an older ball has lost all its shine it can even be persuaded to 'reverse swing'. This is where the bowling team contrives to let one side get extremely rough, causing airflow to become so disrupted that it forces the ball to move in the opposite direction to that expected by a batter studying the bowler's grip. Reverse swing is a fiendish weapon in the pace bowler's armoury because the ball moves later in flight than with conventional swing, reducing the batter's reaction time. Much depends on the bowler's action, the presence of overhead cloud, the humidity and wind conditions and whether the ball is pitched up, giving it more chance to curve through the air. Some days though, no matter what you do, the ball goes ramrod straight.

Spin bowling

You'll often hear commentators talk about spinners as 'magicians'. Looking back on my career, they surely cast their spell on me. I liked the ball coming on to me quickly so that I could use pace off the bat to punch shots through the outfield. But top-class T20 or ODI spinners were a nightmare. I strongly suspected them of sitting in their dressing room before play with a bubbling cauldron on the go and The Big Book of Spinners' Spells in their hands so that, by the time I got to face their bowling, the ball would be possessed by a spiteful, malicious spirit bent on my humiliation. There was so much to think about – the flight of the ball, its speed, how far and which way it would turn off the pitch, whether it would even turn (the 'top-spinner') – and so by the time it came fizzing towards me I'd be agonising and dithering over the correct shot to play. I got better over the years, but it was slow progress.

Off-spin – turning the ball from off to leg – is the most common form of the art among right-handed bowlers. The index and middle fingers are spread across the seam with the ball resting on the third finger and the thumb having little involvement. Spin is generated by turning the wrist and fingers in a clockwise direction – some coaches call this 'opening the door', as if turning a door handle – and the bigger the 'rip' across the seam the greater rotations imparted on the ball. Left-handed finger-spinners use the same technique but turn the ball anti-clockwise, i.e. leg spin to a right-handed batter. Finally, there are the wrist-spinners. They really have come straight from the Gates of Mordor – think Australia's Shane Warne and India's Anil Kumble in the 1990s and 2000s, and England's Adil Rashid or Sri Lanka's Wanindu Hasaranga in today's game. A right-handed wrist-spinner (a misnomer, as the fingers still do most of the work) typically gets the ball breaking from leg to off. The bowler's fingers start on the inside of the ball and naturally cut down the side as the ball is released from the back of the hand.

When T20 cricket was first launched there were fears it would kill the art of spin bowling. Some coaches convinced themselves that spinners would be slogged into submission and that pace bowling was king. In fact, the reverse turned out to be true. In the limited-overs game, match data shows that spinners have come into their own and sit consistently high in the rankings because they provide more control – particularly leg spinners operating in the middle overs of a game. There's no doubt that the introduction of DRS (see H for Howzat), which allows a third umpire to review ball-tracking data, has been a godsend for them. For one thing, it allows a challenge to any umpire who rejects an lbw appeal. It also makes lbw a far greater danger for batters because they can no longer rely on an umpire giving them the benefit of the doubt. The all-seeing tracking software will indicate in seconds whether a ball pitching in line, or outside off, would have hit the stumps if the batter's pads hadn't got in the way. When I started, the technology was still in its infancy so I used to play mind games with umpires by making a great show of taking my guard way outside the crease. The message I hoped to send was: *Hey, look at me, I'm batting way down the pitch. If the ball hits my pad it's got a long way to travel before it gets anywhere near the stumps. Are you really going to give me out lbw?*

Death bowling

Sounds bad, doesn't it? To be clear, 'death' is short for 'at the death', in other words the final few overs of a T20 or a one-day game in which a batting side is looking to slog anything and everything. When I began playing white-ball cricket, the received wisdom was either to send down fast yorkers, trying to land them on your opponent's toes, or slip in slower balls to draw the batter into playing too early. That all changed when the scoop shot came in. We found batters were able to move forward and scoop the ball for boundaries. Tactics became much more cat-and-mouse; you'd go for wide yorkers or bowl consistently on the side of the wicket where your boundary fielders offered most protection. But the game keeps evolving, and batters are smarter now and have a wider range of shots. These days you can't send down identical deliveries back to back, you have to try strategies that would once be considered heretical, such as the slow bouncer, which players like Australia's Ellyse Perry and England's Lauren Bell have perfected in the women's game. Death bowling is one of the most valuable skills in cricket because it comes at a stage when matches are often won or lost.

Bowling variations

A bowler's variation sometimes includes use of the crease, the point at which the ball is released. Normally, she'll try to land her front foot just behind the popping crease (the line parallel to the stumps and 4 ft in front of them). This is the shortest possible distance from which she can deliver a legal ball. But bowlers will sometimes release from a couple of feet behind the popping crease, in other words a greater distance than necessary, to subtly vary their length (see B for Batting). The 2024 T20 Men's World Cup saw Scottish spinner Mark Watt deploy his trademark delivery from a full two yards behind the crease, causing a good old-fashioned rules rumpus during Scotland's Group B game against Oman. Oman's No. 5, Khalid Kail, was looking up in a ready-to-receive stance, his bat was down, and he had no obvious excuse for walking away as Watts's delivery sailed towards him. It crashed into his stumps, whereupon he argued that he wasn't ready, a plea the umpire controversially accepted. It's probably true that Kail didn't think Watt was going to bowl so early, but that was entirely his problem; Watt was in front of the umpire when he released the ball, the ball was live and it was a fair delivery. At the time most commentators thought Kail had got away with one. In the end it mattered little – Scotland won comfortably by seven wickets with 41 balls remaining – but it was a smart tactic from Watt, who was entitled to feel aggrieved. He later made clear he was going to keep the 24-yarder in his armoury – and you can understand why. In the best-case scenario, he gets a wicket. In the worst case, the batter survives but feels unsettled; you've got into his head and sowed uncertainty among his team.

The donkey drop

It's beyond me why this kind of bowling – a ball lobbed high into the air – is linked to donkeys. It looks easy to clatter to the boundary but turns out to be surprisingly tricky. India's Poonam Raut would bowl them at 38 mph, and former England spinner Jeremy Snape, now a sports psychologist, had one he called his moonball – batters just hoped it would land before nightfall. I hated this kind of bowling. I'd play four or five different shots while the ball was in the air before spooning a catch to mid-off. Donkey drops were one of my big weaknesses.

Favourite bowlers – and those I dreaded

I loved seam bowlers who shaped deliveries away from me. This played to my strengths – strong shots, hitting ball through the covers on the front foot or cutting on the back foot. My England team-mate Isa Guha was definitely a favourite bowler to face and there would be predictable banter between us over who'd win the personal battle whenever Surrey played her county side, Berkshire. Obviously she's a mate but, when you're on the pitch in a head-to-head, you want to come out on top. I always felt that Isa would bowl to my sweet spot, although I knew she was a wily, fast-medium opening bowler who could tease out impressive swing – especially late swing, which is so dangerous for a batter. We played a lot of red-ball cricket in those days and that suited her style. Her record also commanded respect. So, while I looked forward to our encounters, there was never anything straightforward about them.

A medium-pace bowler I struggled against was Anya Shrubsole, another England team-mate. She would produce the precise opposite of what I wanted by getting the ball to hit the seam and nip back. Whenever the season's fixtures were published, I'd look down the list, see Somerset, think *here comes Anya*, and know I was going to be severely tested on my weakest skill sets.

Over time I had to learn different techniques to counter bowling that fell outside my comfort zone and my England captain Charlotte Edwards did a great job in helping improve that side of my game. It meant I became more confident in facing arguably the best fast bowlers of all time – players like India's Jhulan Goswami, the Aussies Cathryn Fitzpatrick and Ellyse Perry and our own Katherine Sciver-Brunt. I remember Lottie coaching me to face Goswami, getting me to stand a foot or so outside the crease to try and throw her off course and make her pitch on a nice driveable length for me rather than that 4- to 6-yard area, which is so awkward. I'd also switch my usual middle stump guard to middle-and-leg to offer more width against her away-swing. With Anya I'd tend to do the opposite, a middle-and-off guard that allowed me to hit balls shaping in towards leg. Picking up these little tips and tweaks from the way other batters navigated top-class bowling produced a massive impact on my performance. I wasn't changing my technique, I was just changing the bowler's comfort zone into mine. This works particularly well in the Powerplay (see P) when most fielders are inside the circle.

Spinners I hated facing

Top of this list would be Holly Colvin of Sussex and England. She was a thinking bowler, and I always felt she knew exactly what my game plan was – namely, charging down the pitch to try and stifle the spin on the bounce or drive the ball before it could spin. I would play around 20 different shots in my head, thinking about angles, flight and turn, and all that while the ball was still airborne. Too often, the result was not pretty. Holly could hang the ball in the air or fire it in short without a significant change in her action. She was such a difficult bowler to read and at times I felt like I was playing mouse to her cat. The two overseas spinners I most fretted over were Australia's Shelley Nitschke, also a left-armer, who would dart in ball after ball on off stump. Her consistency was remarkable; she never gave me any width to play the cut shots I liked. Then there was Lisa Sthalekar, like Shelley a true Aussie great of the women's game, who amassed over 200 wickets and almost 3,500 runs in limited-overs cricket over a ten-year career. Lisa flighted the ball brilliantly. As a batter, you want to face a spinner who floats the ball up in a nice arc, just above your eye line, so that it's easy to watch out of the hand and onto your bat. Lisa knew that too, which is why she rarely obliged. She would flight high or fire flat with plenty of teasing variations in between.

Wides and no-balls

These are covered by Laws 21 and 22 for readers who want the complete lowdown. But, put simply, a ball gets called 'wide' if the umpire decides it is directed so far away from the stumps that the batter can't reach it 'by means of a normal cricket stroke'. In limited-overs games this rule is interpreted more strictly than in Test cricket to stop bowlers stifling the scoring with wide deliveries that would – just – be judged legal. T20I and ODI pitches therefore include 'wide line' indicators marked either side of the wickets and 17 in. closer to them than the return crease (see G for Ground). No-balls are all about the position of the bowler's feet and arm during delivery, the height of a full toss, how often the ball bounces before reaching the batter and, in the white-ball game, whether there are too many fielders outside the inner circle (see G for Ground and P for Powerplay).

My old Surrey captain Mel Jones used to spit feathers if we conceded wides, or, worse, no-balls. A wide gives the batting side both an extra run and an extra ball, and the only way of getting out to one is if you're run out, stumped, obstruct the field or hit your wicket (see O for Out). In my view there are only three occasions where 'strategic' wides are acceptable in limited-overs cricket. The first is if you're trying to bowl an off-side yorker to force the batter into hitting towards fielders patrolling that side of the outfield (sometimes your delivery creeps over the wide line). The second is where a batter is charging down the pitch to throw you off your length. In that case, you might try bowling wider down the leg side, making it harder for the charging batter to make contact and providing your keeper with a stumping chance. The third is the slow bouncer, often an effective variation, which goes slightly wrong. These are all strategic ploys but repeatedly bowling poor, wide deliveries is taboo.

Free hits

Like wides, no-balls incur a penalty run against the fielding team, along with an extra ball. There are only three ways of getting out to one – run out, obstructing the field or hitting the ball twice – so you might as well have a good risk-free whack at any no-ball called because you can score more runs in addition to the penalty. That's the overriding rule for Test and red-ball county matches, but in limited-overs cricket the consequences are more damaging: the batting side not only gets the penalty run and any further runs tacked on, but the extra ball counts as a 'free hit'. This gives the batter on strike the same immunity to dismissal as a no-ball and effectively offers a pre-planned, risk-free chance to smash a four or six. Provided that batter faced the original no-ball, fielders aren't even allowed to change position – they can't head to the boundary to protect it.

Without wishing to immerse readers in the weeds of this rule, it is worth mentioning novel ways that batters can take advantage. If a free-hit ball strikes the stumps and cannons off into the outfield, the batting side can take runs as though the ball was struck with the bat. It's the only scenario in cricket where you can be 'bowled' and still score towards your personal total (provided you were on strike for the original no-ball offence). In January 2005, the early days of the T20 format, Australian wicket-keeper Brad Haddin was playing for Australia A against Pakistan at Adelaide when in the first over he was presented with a free hit against Pakistan's Shoaib Akhtar, aka the Rawalpindi Express. Three years earlier, Akhtar had bowled the fastest delivery ever recorded in cricket, 100.2 mph, and Haddin rightly concluded that his free hit would give him more time to see the ball. As Akhtar released, Haddin – knowing he could not be bowled – stepped a yard behind the stumps and hit the ball for two runs (a perfectly legal shot). That delivery was again called no-ball, which meant a second free hit. Once more Haddin stepped behind the stumps, but this time Akhtar's ball smashed into them and ricocheted into the outfield. Haddin ran what was then recorded as a bye, although under new ICC rules it would today have counted towards his personal score. He was out for two, almost certainly the most eventful two of his career, as Akhtar bowled him with the fifth legal delivery of the over.

Tours

My first overseas tournament for England was that 2006–7 ICC Women's 50-over quadrangular series in Chennai. We were competing against India, New Zealand and the best team in the world at that time, Australia. Their deadliest weapon was Cathryn Fitzpatrick, the fastest bowler in women's cricket and not one to take prisoners. As well as being quick, she was accurate and aggressive – everything you'd want in a strike bowler – and Australia were soon all over us. I fancied myself as a batter but I wasn't seen at this stage in my career as a top-order player. So when I went in at 165 for seven with eight overs remaining, I told myself we'd lost a lot of wickets and we needed runs, so why not try to impress the coaches by playing a few shots? It started OK – quick hands through the shot, a couple of nice drives – although I kept hitting the ball straight to fielders. Nonetheless, I thought: *OK, Fitzpatrick, I've got this.* Then she just dragged the length back, bent her back and suddenly – although it was a slow pitch – her shorter ball spat up at me. It beat me for pace, leaving me helicoptering nowhere near it. It made me think: *Am I ready for this level? Do I really want to take on the quickest bowler in the world?* It was humbling, get-back-in-your box moment, a sharp reminder that great international bowlers work you out very quickly. Cathryn didn't sledge me; I don't think I was a valuable enough player, which in some ways made it even worse. I wasn't decent enough for her to bother with words. I just slunk back in my crease and avoided eye contact.

Tour parties (don't get caught)

Women cricketers on tour don't get up to the wilder antics you see from the men. At least, not in my experience. Nonetheless, we have our moments and you sometimes need to let off steam to give yourself a break from the intensity of professional sport. Trouble is, there are always consequences. At the end of our 2009–10 tour of the West Indies, the one where we lost the ODI and the T20I series 2–1 2–1, despite being world champions, the mood in the camp was pretty dire. Our coach, Mark Lane, was seriously pissed off and ordered everyone onto the team bus and straight back to our hotel. He made clear there would be no partying if he had anything to do with it. We were staying in Saint Kitts and on the journey back I couldn't help but notice these great little beach bars lining the route. I said to the girls: 'Look, the tour's over. We can't do any worse. We're not flying home for a day or so. We might as well have a night out to cheer ourselves up.' I got Katherine Sciver-Brunt and Isa Guha onside and within a few minutes the entire squad had signed up – even Beth Morgan, who was always the quiet one. As we arrived at the hotel, we all stood up in the bus to see Mark already on his feet. 'A reminder, girls,' he piped up ominously, 'that we have individual tour-reflection meetings in the morning. Please be prompt.' Mark knew I liked to party and that if something was being cooked up, I'd probably be behind it. As I walked past him, he flourished his schedule for the reflection chats and pointed to my name. Inevitably I was up first. I insisted it would be no problem and promised we'd all be back by 10pm that evening. That obviously didn't happen. I saw the girls put away jaw-dropping quantities of vanilla rum and we eventually tipped up back at the hotel as breakfast was being served. I had no time to change and walked, unsteadily, straight to the interview room, where I sat down a little too abruptly. Mark gave me a long look. Then: 'What are your reflections on the tour, Ebony?' As he said that, a large dollop of sand plopped out of the bottom of my trousers onto the carpet between us. We both stared at it. Mark broke the silence: 'Quiet night, was it?'

My favourite tour prank

This was a Jenny Gunn wind-up aimed at Danni Wyatt-Hodge, who was on her first tour. The whole team were in on it. Before every foreign trip we'd be advised by our medical people to be cautious about everything we ate and drank. You can pick up a tummy bug anywhere, it's no different to being on holiday, but the last thing you want is to get ill directly before a game. So Jenny had an eager pair of ears in Danni. When we arrived in India, she mentioned that all the girls took particular care while showering because it might not be drinking water coming out of the nozzle. She said the best precaution was to get hold of a Tubigrip – the elasticated tubes players normally pull onto their arm as a support for stresses and strains – and pull it right down over her face while under the shower. That way she could be sure no water got into her mouth. The rest of us nodded sagely at this and confirmed it was best practice, in fact a complete no-brainer during tours.

Danni decided that if everyone else did this, she'd follow suit. We all had a quiet laugh but thought no more of it until, some four weeks later she stormed into the gym, brandishing a Tubigrip and shouting: 'Guys, I can't do this anymore. I've had enough. I don't care what the water's like, I can't shower like this.' Incredibly, she'd stuck with Jenny's advice every time she showered. It was a bit of an initiation. Fair play to Danni, she was stitched up but took it well.

TMS on tour

My first men's overseas tour as a *Test Match Special* summariser left me with a memory that still gives me nightmares. I'd joined Jonathan Agnew and the team for the T20 World Cup in Bangladesh 2014 with a brief to provide quality in-play analysis and insight. We were on air for one of the T20 games, Aggers was providing his usual consummate commentary, and I was occasionally filling the gaps. At one point, for reasons unclear to me, I drifted off into a reverie and only gradually became aware that he was speaking directly to me. 'What do you think, Ebony?' What did I think about what? A question from Aggers on TMS could be anything from the quality of last night's curry to something requiring an incisive comment. I took a gamble. 'Do you know what,' I replied sagely, 'just twat it.' I have no idea whether this had any relevance to our conversation, and Aggers – bless him – somehow managed to gloss over it. Afterwards I got a severe telling-off from producer Adam Mountford, and rightly so.

Aggers got me out of a hole in Bangladesh but I knew it wouldn't be long before he tried to stitch me up on air. Every TMS listener and show pundit knows he has form for this, going back decades. Sure enough, his opportunity came the following year when we were on air together. He delightedly regaled me with a story he'd seen in the newspapers, revealing that the Dorset Knob, a traditional hard biscuit first baked during the nineteenth century, was being used to help raise money for village amenities in the West Dorset village of Cattistock. Villagers had arranged a 'Knob Throwing Contest' in which contestants competed to see how far they could throw a Knob. One of the beneficiaries of this event was Cattistock Cricket Club, providing the perfect excuse for Jonathan to raise the subject with me. 'Ebony,' he enquired innocently, 'have you ever had a Dorset Knob?' I could see what was happening here but opted to play it straight. 'I haven't,' I replied cautiously, 'what are they?' Aggers was in his element: 'They're really firm and hard – you'd enjoy eating one, I'm absolutely certain of it.' I sat there quietly for the rest of the over, noting from the TMS schedule in front of us that I was about to finish my stint in the commentary box and be replaced by another summariser. This was the moment. 'Aggers,' I said, 'I'm sure I'd love a good hard Knob in the morning.' Whereupon I hotfooted it out of the box, leaving him to burble alone on the mic. It was a proud moment in my early broadcasting career – the arch-stitcher, stitched up.

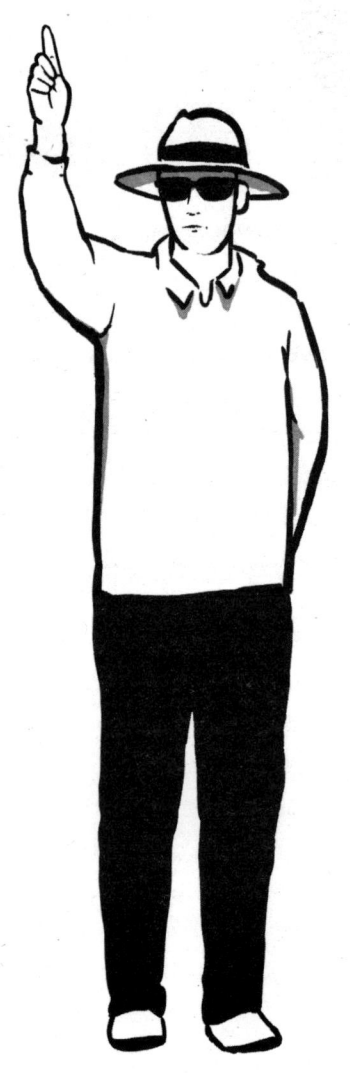

Umpires

Any batter can have a bad day with umpires. My worst came late in my playing career while I was playing for Shepperton, a club to which several of the England girls had gravitated. We were batting against a Hampshire side known on the circuit for deploying somewhat biased match officials (in those days each club appointed their own) and I'd opened with another Surrey girl, Holly Knight. We were smashing the bowling around the park – I know that sounds arrogant, but we were taking them down. Then this girl sent down the worst delivery I've ever faced in my life. It was on a par with the infamous wide bowled by Steve Harmison, the first ball of that calamitous 2006–7 Ashes series in Australia in which England were whitewashed 5–0. This one started on the line of second slip and was parried even further wide by the keeper as she dived to prevent four byes. It ended up in the hands of gully. I didn't even try to play a shot. I just walked away, thinking: *this is awful*.

Next thing I know, the keeper is screaming: 'Howzat?' I replied: 'How's what?' and both Holly and I started laughing. We genuinely thought it was a joke. But then I spotted that the umpire had his finger up. I'm standing there and either the keeper or first slip chirps up: 'Bitch, if he gives you out, get out.' And I properly lost it. I sprayed everyone with a diatribe of choice language covering everything from the spirit of cricket to how umpires can live with themselves if they cheat so outrageously. It went on for some time until one of my team-mates came onto the outfield to drag me away. But it didn't end there; I was still chuntering away in the pavilion – this time at the square-leg who at least had the grace to look embarrassed but offered nothing more than a shrug in return. I knew that, because I'd sworn at least twice at the umpire and my opponents, I would be in serious trouble.

Sure enough, I then got a sniffy letter from the ECB, telling me that as an England player and role model for youngsters I'd let women's cricket down, broken basic disciplinary rules and would be banned for two matches. The irony was that I'd had a squeaky-clean career in which I'd never faced disciplinary action. I was wrong to react as I did, and I accepted the ban, but I also wrote back a four-page letter questioning how such bad cheating could ever be seen as upholding the spirit of cricket. The other club gave their view of things – the umpire claimed a bead of sweat had dropped in his eye and he couldn't see properly. He'd looked down to wipe it away, missed what happened and then couldn't understand how the ball was caught by gully unless I'd hit it there. How absurd is that? As an umpire, how can you give anyone out unless you've seen the full passage of play? These are the joys of club cricket. Looking back, it's clear to me that they were out to get us. From their perspective, we were England internationals, off playing elite cricket for most of the season and now swaggering back to show the girls in club cricket how it's done. Everyone hates a ringer, a player who has no real connection to a team but has been brought in, often from overseas, to help secure a few wins. We must have looked like a team of ringers.

Umpires, overthrows and the greatest ODI ever

The attempted run-out of Ben Stokes in the 2019 Men's World Cup final was one of cricket's greatest controversies in what many commentators argue was the greatest ODI of all time. It culminated in an umpiring error that allowed England the chance to win the World Cup after they seemed dead and buried. Where to begin? If a ball fired in by a fielder hits my bat as I'm trying to make my ground, and gets diverted for overthrows, that's fine by me. Provided I've made no deliberate attempt to knock the ball away, those extra runs are the fielding side's problem. I know there are mixed views on this – some will say it's against the spirit of cricket – but as far as I'm concerned, I've done nothing wrong. When taking a run, batters are entitled to follow a line that puts themselves between the target stumps and the throwing fielder. That's sensible and good practice as long as they don't change course halfway through and risk getting out, obstructing the field, as mentioned in our Jason Roy example in O for Out. It's exactly what Stokes did as he turned for a second run in that final over of the 2019 World Cup final. He wasn't looking at the fielder, the ball hit his bat, it was clearly not deliberate and it ricocheted for four overthrows. He apologised to the Kiwis, although he had nothing to apologise for. It was just bad luck. He even asked the umpires to subtract the four runs from England's score, but they couldn't do that because it was too late and the Laws don't allow it. So, together with the two he'd apparently just run, Stokes had added six to his side's score, leaving England three runs to win off the final two balls of their innings (we'll come to that in a moment).

The bizarre twist to this extraordinary drama is that, in a heartbeat, umpires Kumar Dharmasena and Marais Erasmus made both right and wrong decisions. They were right to award the four but wrong to award the two. Here's why: Law 19.8 (overthrow or wilful act of fielder) states that, in the event of a boundary resulting from an overthrow, the batting side scores the boundary 'and the runs completed by the batsmen, together with the run in progress, if they had already crossed at the instant of the throw.' And there's the rub: Dharmasena and Erasmus thought Stokes and his partner, Asil Rashid, had indeed crossed as the throw came in. Except TV replays proved they hadn't. Stokes and Rashid had therefore completed only one run – making a five instead of a six. But the game had already moved on and it was seemingly too late to knock off an England run.

Who knows what might have happened had the hosts been denied that extra run? As it was, they managed only two more off the two remaining balls as first Rashid then Mark Wood got run out while trying to take dodgy second runs. With the scores tied at 241, the game went to a Super Over (see glossary) but that also ended in a tie. At which point the ICC tournament director invoked the 'boundary countback' rule as a final tie-breaker, with the side scoring the most boundaries declared the winner. This gave England the trophy, 26 to 17, with the Black Caps left to wonder what might have been had Stokes's six been properly called as a five. You have to say that, despite it all, captain Kane Williamson's side were magnificent in the sporting way they accepted defeat. Whatever the tournament rules may have said, there was nothing between these two sides.

Lbws and foxing the umpire

At international level the use of ball-tracking technology (see H for Howzat) has removed any dispute over lbw decisions. The database records hundreds of thousands of deliveries, logging the bowler's action, line, length and degree of bounce to determine precisely whether a ball would have gone on to hit the stumps. In village and club cricket, though, lbw verdicts are solely down to the on-field umpire. Batters hearing gleeful 'howzat' cries will often seek to game the decision-making process, either by stepping quickly away so that an umpire can't line up ball, pads and stumps or by exaggerated grinning at the ridiculous notion that such an appeal could possibly be valid. Another trick is to make it emphatically clear from the start of your innings that you've taken your guard a long way out of your crease. That signals to the umpire that any ball hitting your pads will still have some way to travel before reaching the stumps, establishing some uncertainty in the line and height of bounce. Be warned, though, a guard way outside the crease isn't a good idea against a canny spinner; you're asking to be stumped.

The Duckworth–Lewis–Stern method

We've got to U in my A–Z without mentioning the Duckworth–Lewis–Stern method but the moment can be delayed no longer. This system, named after the mathematicians who devised and adapted it, was first introduced into limited-overs cricket in 1997 as a way of producing a fair result when rain or bad light caused overs to be lost during play. It involves assigning values to constantly changing 'assets' possessed by the team batting second as they chase down their target score, i.e. one more than their opponents' total. They have two assets – wickets remaining and overs remaining – and so, when overs are lost, both assets are used to calculate a reduced target. Some clever sums are required; it's not as straightforward as simply taking runs off the team who batted first in proportion to the number of overs lost. That's because a team batting second with eight wickets intact and 15 overs left can risk more expansive shots from more accomplished batters than a team with only four wickets left in the same circumstances. Provided at least 20 overs are bowled (this is the minimum that constitutes a game), Duckworth–Lewis–Stern seeks to set the chasing team a reduced target that represents the same degree of difficulty as their original one.

Initially, teams struggled to grasp the implications of a Duckworth–Lewis intervention (you can perhaps see why) and there were some high-profile blunders. Perhaps the most gut-wrenching occurred during a Pool B World Cup qualifying match in March 2003 as tournament hosts South Africa took on Sri Lanka. Rain reduced the available overs from 50 to 45, with the Proteas' target cut from 269 to 229. It seemed as though batters Mark Boucher and Shaun Pollock's stand of 63 had taken their team to the brink of victory, but further rain was threatening and twelfth man (see glossary) Nicky Boje was dispatched onto the outfield to make sure Boucher and his new partner Lance Klusener understood what was required. From this point on, accounts differ. The South Africa camp later accused the umpires of hustling Boje away before he had a chance to spell it out. Other reports claimed Boucher's team-mates didn't understand that the Duckworth–Lewis formula produced the target for a tie rather than a win. Boucher smashed a six off the penultimate delivery and then, wrongly believing the job was done, blocked out the final ball. That meant the game was tied, with each side awarded two points. It wasn't enough for the hosts to qualify and so Sri Lanka, New Zealand and Kenya went through to the knock-out stage. South Africa were left to reflect on having ejected themselves from their own World Cup.

These days scorers, dressing rooms and media pundits all have access to computer readouts that instantly report, ball by ball, what a team needs to do to win under the Duckworth–Lewis method. This has produced a new set of problems because struggling teams can leverage that knowledge to their advantage by deploying some distinctly dark arts such as slowing the over rate down, or checking the rain radar and hoping that bad light or a promised cloudburst comes in time to ensure the game is abandoned on grounds of insufficient overs bowled. This was clearly England's thinking as they blatantly attempted to slow play down during the rain-affected final ODI of the 2024 series against Australia at Bristol. With the Aussies batting second, and well ahead of their Duckworth–Lewis target, the hosts were hoping further rain would arrive before the minimum 20 overs could be bowled. At one point, bowler Matthew Potts managed to waste almost three minutes by insisting he needed to change a damaged boot. In the end, the rain arrived four balls into the 21st over, with Australia 49 runs ahead under the Duckworth–Lewis formula, sufficient to win the series 3–2.

V

Village Cricket

While I've never played much village cricket, I've been involved in plenty of charity games in which dubious ability defines the day. Still, it's comforting to discover that planting your boot in the way of a cover drive is considered an acceptable fielding technique; you no longer need to be the only one sliding in to collect the ball. It's true that some fielders will go to ground in the cause of preventing runs, but I'd describe their efforts as more of a flop than a dive. You also encounter the 'tactical flop', typically wheeled out when a well-built player realises there's a risk of having to chase the ball to a distant boundary. Far easier to flop from distance as it whizzes past and inform sceptical team-mates that you 'nearly got to it'. Another favourite spectacle is to watch a 'rusty' bowler deliver the ball backwards – hard to do deliberately – and see it landing behind the non-striker's stumps or even the far reaches of the outfield. Finally, there's nothing better than observing a once-a-year cricketer get hit in the box by a cricket ball. That may sound cruel and uncaring but it always produces unrestrained hilarity, especially among the poor unfortunate's team-mates. I can say all this because I've embarrassed myself so many times on a cricket field. It's all part of the wonderful culture of our sport. If anyone owns the game, it's the people who turn out without fail on village greens and dodgy park pitches the length and breadth of the country, give it their all and retire wearily to the pub afterwards to recount what might have been.

For some it will have been a miserable day in the middle – out for a duck; bowling dispatched to all corners of the ground; easy catches dropped – with a decent home-made tea laid out in the pavilion the only consolation. Fortunately, one of cricket's unwritten laws is that a generous hunk of cake invariably lifts the spirits.

Teas – angel cake

Throughout my career, angel cake has always been a life-saver. I could never resist the look of that pink, yellow and plain sponge combo. I'd load up with at least a couple for club games and Young England training sessions and scoff the lot. I was selfish about it. I wasn't in the business of handing round slices to team-mates. The nutritionists would explain why it was a bad idea, but I never listened until I was selected for England B against the Netherlands. That was a big day, my first representative game for my country, and big days call for extra angel cake, so I popped three into my kit bag. Unfortunately, our coach Charlotte Dickenson had been warned about my predilection and her first words to me were: 'No angel cake today, Ebony.' I took that as a light-hearted aside. This was, after all, the cake that gave me my mojo. At lunch, I was getting stuck in when Charlotte came up behind me and without warning smashed her fist into my cake, pounding it into oblivion in front of everyone. I was devastated but afterwards one of the selectors called me over and said: 'Look, cake may be fine at club level but you're an international now. Eat properly.' That was the end of it. I went cold turkey and I haven't bought angel cake since. At the time I compensated with extreme tea-drinking, only to find it caused acid reflux that meant I had to detox from caffeine for six months. After that, lunch and tea breaks were all protein shakes, cereal bars and bananas. I do still hanker after a good cricket tea, preferably with a slice of something that tastes like an angel crying on your tongue. Especially if there's seconds.

Willow

There are two key things about bats: one is the science of their construction (where the weight is concentrated, the edge thickness, the sweet spot in the middle, the drying process and moisture retention of the willow); the other is simply how they feel in your hands. Sometimes you'll pick up a bat and the backlift is effortless. In my playing days you could hand me a dozen and I'd tell you the precise weight of each. I accept that I was obsessed. I once offered a guy, a total stranger, £300 to buy his bat after watching him practice for an hour in the nets. He didn't sell.

I had custom-made ones from around the age of 15 but I would constantly be on the lookout for more, trying to find that elusive, perfect blade. I would generally opt for a short-handled men's bat and ask the manufacturer to nip a few centimetres more off the top as this suited my grip and stance and reduced the overall weight. I'd also have three slightly different weights so that I could choose whichever best suited pitch conditions on any given day. If I needed more hand speed on a fast wicket I'd go for a 2 lb 5 oz or a 2 lb 6 oz bat, but if it appeared that the ball wouldn't be coming on I'd go 2 lb 6 oz or 2 lb 7 oz to get more energy flowing through the shot. Some male players now use 3 lb bats to make the most of their power-game. I have no idea how they wield those things.

Edging your bets

Most men want the weight towards the lower end of the blade, where they think they can exert the most power. At first, I preferred it in the middle because the balance is better and it suited my favourite cut, pull and drive shots. Later in my career I went for bigger but lighter bats with much thicker edges. The dimensions of a bat have always been regulated but manufacturers discovered they could thicken the edges, increasing the power even of mistimed shots, while staying within the rules and maintaining overall weight. They did this by further drying out the willow, but in the end the edges became ridiculous and lawmakers at MCC decided things had to be reined in. In 2017 the maximum dimensions for a bat became 4.33 in. width, 2.68 in. depth and 1.61 in. for edges.

Looking back, it's amazing how much has changed in the way bats are made and maintained. When I started, you would lovingly coat them with linseed oil and knock them in with a bat mallet to press the fibres together and make the surface harder. It could take a whole season to knock your bat in – hours of your life you'll never get back – but they lasted years. My first bat, a Stuart Surridge, is exhibited in Surrey CC's museum. I could take it out tomorrow, hit balls in the nets all season and it would be fine. Later, bats would leave factories as humungous pieces of willow that weighed next to nothing and were pre-knocked in by machine. They would be match-ready from the get-go but you'd break at least two every season. The last bat I used will now be very brittle and might struggle to get through a single net session against quick bowling. The difference between them is extraordinary: one thin and dense, the other massive and light.

X-Factor XIs

I'm going to get some stick for this section so, to paraphrase the Irish rugby legend Willie John McBride, I'm getting my retaliation in first. There's a pub game – cricketers rarely do anything in a parlour – where you select teams comprising the best players ever to take the field. You pretend they all played concurrently and then argue about whose selection would win in matches against the others. Pointless, of course, but it passes the time. Rather than try to pick the 'best' XI here, I've picked out 'X-factor' players who would lift a side by their very presence, whether it be through strength of character, exceptional skill or proven ability in all conditions against the very best opponents. Looking down the lists, quite a few tick all three boxes.

X-factor men's XI

Don Bradman, Australia
I can't leave The Don out. His Test match batting average of 99.94 between 1928 and 1948 is unmatched and his consistency supports the argument that he's the greatest sportsperson ever. Australians certainly think so.

Chris Gayle, West Indies
Gayle's nickname among West Indian cricket fans is 'the Universe Boss', which just seems a longer way of calling him 'God'. He has the stats distinction of an extraordinary treble: a triple hundred in Test matches, a double in ODIs and a plain old century in T20Is.

Viv Richards (captain), West Indies
Viv Richards's flair made him one of cricket's great entertainers. He was a game-changer and his 121 Tests produced an outstanding batting average of 50.24. He won 27 of the 50 matches he captained – a great return in an era of draws.

Sachin Tendulkar, India
The most technically gifted batter of my lifetime, he is the highest run-scorer in the history of both Test and ODI cricket, with a combined total of 34,357 runs over a 14-year career. Kumar Sangakkara, a fabulous wicketkeeper-batter, comes in second, over 6,000 runs behind. Mentally resilient, Tendulkar almost always delivered.

Brian Lara, West Indies
The most graceful of players, his technique and dogged concentration made him the greatest left-hander of his generation. Muttiah Muralitharan regarded the Trinidadian as his toughest opponent, and anyone in the England team unfortunate enough to be fielding as he hit the highest individual Test score in history – 400 not out in 2004 – will probably agree.

Jacques Kallis, South Africa
Maybe he wasn't the most stylish player. But Kallis's X-factor was his ability to galvanise a team under any circumstances.

The all-rounder is the only cricketer to have scored more than 10,000 runs and taken over 250 wickets in both Test and ODI formats. By the way, he was a brilliant fielder too.

Adam Gilchrist (wicket-keeper), Australia

If you could point to one player who truly revolutionised the Test wicket-keeper role, it would have to be Gilchrist. He was an explosive batter who would rather have walked across hot coals than play a forward-defensive. Gilchrist forced selectors to reassess how keepers balanced a batting line-up.

Shane Warne, Australia

Warne defined the art of leg spin. Hyperbole is an affliction of sports journalism, but his 'ball of the century' in 1993 to dismiss Mike Gatting – Warne's first ball in an Ashes Test – merited the description. His total of 708 Test and 293 ODI wickets is bettered only by Muralitharan.

Wasim Akram, Pakistan

One of the great left-arm pace bowlers. His ability to produce reverse swing and in-swinging, toe-crunching, yorkers was lethal. Wasim's buttery-smooth action changed the dynamic of how fast bowlers learn their craft.

Mark Wood, England

This is an X-factor team and extreme pace is a rare and precious cricketing asset. I'll accept accusations of English bias but, with a top speed of almost 98 mph, Wood can trouble any batter in the world. He's bowled the fastest over ever recorded by an Englishman.

Muttiah Muralitharan, Sri Lanka
The most feared of spinners, his unorthodox bowling style and range of deliveries made him unique. No one even comes close to his tally of 800 Test and 534 ODI wickets. What else can you say?

Gary Sobers (twelfth man), West Indies
Another fabulously graceful cricketer. His career stats (8,032 Test runs at an average of 57.78, and 235 wickets at 34.03) make him one of the true greats, but Kallis just pips him for my all-rounder berth.

X-factor women's XI

Charlotte Edwards (captain), England
An outstanding batter and brilliant captain throughout her 20-year career. She is England Women's all-time highest run-scorer in T20s and ODIs, and as captain brought home two World Cups and three Ashes triumphs.

Chamari Athapaththu, Sri Lanka
One of the most valuable players across all formats of the global game. At the time of writing, her T20 strike rate (runs per 100 balls) of 110.01 is nothing short of ridiculous.

Karen Rolton, Australia
I grew up idolising her. Karen was a destructive left-handed batter who took sides apart and helped ensure Australia dominated the game for years. When she arrived on the scene, women weren't scoring at pace. She changed that mindset.

Sarah Taylor (wicket-keeper), England

The most gifted keeper the women's game has ever seen. Fact. She had natural flair with the bat. It's no surprise that she was snapped up to coach in the men's game.

Ellyse Perry, Australia

A global icon of the women's game and probably its first superstar. That breakthrough was important. Perry was a consummate all-rounder who bowled high 70s and oozed consistency with the bat, averaging 61 in Tests, 50 in ODIs and 31 in T20s.

Deandra Dottin, West Indies

Another brilliant all-rounder. She is the first woman to score a T20 century, is a proven World Cup six-hitter, bowls lethal yorkers at the death and is arguably the best fielder in the game.

Marizanne Kapp, South Africa

A new-ball specialist who shapes the ball in flight better than anyone. She's a great athlete, dynamic in the field, and her middle-order batting can steady the ship in the event of early wickets tumbling.

Enid Blakewell, England

England's greatest all-rounder. During the 1960s and 1970s she was the equivalent of Don Bradman in the women's game, and I'm proud to say I played in the same team as her after she retired. (She was EB1 and I was EB2, a play on us possessing the same initials.) She took 75 wickets in Tests and ODIs and hit 1,078 runs with a batting average of 59.88.

Sana Mir, Pakistan
One of Pakistan's longest-serving captains and the country's first woman to take 100 ODI wickets. A canny off-spinner (I well remember her getting me out), she was rarely out of the ICC's top-20 ODI bowler rankings.

Cathryn Fitzpatrick, Australia
The greatest fast bowler in the history of the women's game. She took 60 wickets in 134 Tests at 19.11, and 180 wickets in 109 ODIs at 16.79. With stats like that, she picks herself.

Jhulan Goswami, India
Another towering figure of the women's game (literally, as she was over 6 ft tall). Throughout her 20-year international career Goswami was quick, uncannily accurate and moved the ball both ways. India even issued a postage stamp in her honour.

Belinda Clark (twelfth woman), Australia
One of the great captains, she was the first to score a double century in ODIs.

Yips

The yips is sporting jargon that first seems to have surfaced in golf. It's attributed to a player who, for no obvious reason, suddenly seems unable to hit a putt straight or with the correct weight, or whose swing has fallen apart. I'm no psychologist and I've never seen a definitive explanation of what causes it, but one theory suggests it may be a fear of letting go of the ball. In cricket it tends to affect spin bowlers more than the quicks, perhaps because they have more time to think as they approach the wicket. Whatever the underlying reason, the yips are notoriously difficult to cure.

At Surrey, I remember one young male spin bowler who never managed to overcome them. The guy was considered one of the most talented, up-and-coming spinners in the country with a pro career ahead. Then, in his late teens, he had a growth spurt that meant he released the ball from a greater and greater height. You might think an inch or two would make no difference but, if the ball is travelling 16–18 yards, it is inevitably going to start landing outside your preferred length. You overcorrect, you feel the pressure of needing to impress because contracts are being handed out, and then what started as a small problem ends up feeling huge. That guy, who once had total control, fell apart. It was horrible. He'd be bowling in the nets and the ball would come out backwards or land on top. He had no idea where it was going, none of the coaches could help and it was like his brain had disassociated from the very act of bowling.

I recall it happening a few times to young spinners in friendly games, and umpires would cancel an over if it became clear the bowler had lost all control. It should be said that most youngsters adjust to a growth spurt, practise their way through it and find everything clicks. Coaches understand that and allow space for it to happen. Counties now take the growth potential of their young players seriously – there's a whole science to this, which involves things like predicting their future height from their parents' height or even the length of their toes. The numbers can indicate whether someone is likely to face a sudden growth spurt.

In my early career this kind of analysis never happened and I can't recall anyone coming back from a severe attack of the yips. As for that young lad at Surrey, he sadly never did land a contract.

Z

Zero

Cricket can be the cruellest of sports, whatever the level, especially for batters. You're looking forward to your game, you've practised shots in front of the mirror, done ostentatious warm-ups at the ground, adopted a look of devoted concentration for your captain's team talk, got into the zone mentally while checking the quality of the teatime egg sandwiches, and then out you stride to take your guard, flashing a friendly smile at the umpire (you never know, it might help) before pausing dramatically for a glance around the outfield. The message you're sending is clear: *Do your worst, bowler. I'm hunting boundaries.* And down comes the first ball, swinging, seaming, spitting off the surface, eluding your signature forward-defensive shot and clattering your stumps. You stand, incredulous, staring down at the pitch (it's always the fault of the pitch) before turning for the long trudge back to the pavilion where, depending on the importance of the match, either stifled sniggers or insincere condolences await. And that's your sporting day over: in action for 0.2 seconds, a score of zero, a pariah in the changing room, your rubbish shot playing over and over in your head as you later run around, unsuccessfully chasing opponents' boundaries. However you dress it up, you've failed in your job. Everyone knows it and, unless you're an all-rounder or wicket-keeper, your chances of receiving absolution by contributing something to your team's performance are limited – especially when your skipper has you permanently fielding at fine leg as a punishment. Even the egg sarnies (curling by the time you get to them) appear judgemental.

Whether you're a professional or a once-a-season village occasional, you never signed up for this. Golden ducks are the worst feeling in the world – first ball, snick, out – and a big, fat, round zero nestling against your name in the scorebook for eternity. Cricket is my great love, but I can think of no other team sport that treats its participants, particularly batters, so brutally. As a bowler, you can serve up an over of tripe, only to be instantly forgiven when you get a vital wicket. Score a horrible own goal at football and you might later clear a shot off the line or even score yourself. Rugby, basketball, hockey – all of them offer you a decent chance to make amends. This is why batters need robust mental strength, especially when they're trying to shrug off a run of poor form. If you're playing and missing, it's easy to start hearing the demons of self-doubt in your head, and those voices only get louder. In my teens, coaches would pose the question: 'If you've played and missed at a ball, what can you do about it?' I'd come up with various analytical ideas but the answer was obvious: nothing; the moment's gone so don't dwell on it. Instead, fall back on your technique and your preparation and focus on the next delivery. If ever I played and missed, I would walk towards square leg while the fielders returned the ball to the bowler. That gave me a few seconds to think about any mistake, note it, pack it up, park it and leave it out there. Back at the crease, the rogue shot was history. No point standing at the wicket and playing supposedly better versions of it through the air.

My debut ducks

If I seem passionate about all this it's because I am. I know about ducks. More precisely, I believe I hold the most unenviable ducks record of any debut batter in any international limited-overs game, men or women. It was August 2008, England were playing South Africa in a three-match T20 series at Northampton and all three games were scheduled over two days. We had a newly appointed assistant coach, Jack Birkenshaw, a former England, Yorkshire and Leicestershire spinning legend with a shedload of experience. I was batting No. 7 and, as debutante, I was understandably desperate to impress. When my turn came, he called me over and in his strong Yorkshire accent advised: 'Swing from your bootlaces, lass, swing from your bootlaces.' I wasn't exactly sure what that meant but it was the last over and boundaries were required. I tried to smash a ball from Charlize van der Westhuizen, only to miss it by miles and have my stumps comprehensively rearranged. At which point my international T20 batting figures read: 'Balls faced: 1, Runs: 0, How out: Bowled'. It was a shocker but, on the upside, I told myself that lots of lower-order batters come in right at the death with only a few balls to spare. They're expected to take risks and have a go. Everyone understands that and any player could suffer a similar fate. Besides, we'd won and for me things could only get better.

We played the next match of the series immediately. I was heartened to be batting at No. 6 and as I headed out at 54 for four, it dawned on me that this was a great opportunity to impress – particularly as my captain Charlotte Edwards was on strike at the other end. While we weren't in a great position, it was recoverable and I had a little more time to show off my skill set. Charlotte gave me her traditional greeting of 'alright, mate' (she said 'mate' a lot and I ended up copying her accent) and warned me to run every ball because we needed to up the score. Lottie won't mind me saying this, but she wasn't the quickest between the wickets. Nonetheless, she'd told me to run everything so, when I saw her nudge the ball a few yards, I hared off towards her. I was three-quarters of the way down the wicket when she looked up and shouted: 'Nah, I'm alright', meaning she'd decided to stay in her crease and that I should get back. Of course that meant I was very much not alright. I pleaded 'Lottie?' but she repeated: 'I'm alright.' Obviously I didn't want to run out the in-form batter (and it's just as well I didn't because she went on to rescue us with 76 not out); if anyone was to be sacrificed, it would be me. All I could do was peg it back to my crease. But at that point in my career I didn't have the diving or sliding-in skills to make it. The media photos showed me in a hot mess, diving clumsily, rolling around on the ground, arms and legs flailing, bum in the air and wicket-keeper Daleen Terblanche demolishing the stumps. It was painful to see. It left us at 54 for five, soon to be 60 for six, but we eventually posted 116, which proved enough to win the game and series.

Process not outcome

Now my international record stood at two balls, two ducks. A real impact. The following day the coaches took pity on me – the feeling was that I'd been slightly stitched up – and so, with the series a dead rubber, there was no harm in promoting me. I would be opening the innings with Sarah Taylor, the best steadying influence anyone could ask for, but two ducks had left me more nervous than I'd ever been on a cricket pitch. I lasted six balls for no runs before van der Westhuizen shaped one in and got me lbw. Three international innings, three ducks, all inside 24 hours. No one is ever going to match that, and my team-mates were in stitches as they helpfully pointed it out. Friends and colleagues still wind me up about it today but it's a record I'm happy to own. It's cricket. Sometimes it's your day and sometimes it's not. And sometimes the not-your-days just form a queue.

My mentor in helping deal with this was Alec Stewart, unquestionably one of England's greatest opening batters in Tests and ODIs. At Surrey, Alec worked with me to counter self-doubt, and his mantra was simple: focus on process not outcome. When you start your professional career you're obsessed with outcomes. You're constantly looking up at the scoreboard – how many runs have you got? How many wickets have you taken? These stats matter, of course, but they're not necessarily reliable indicators of underlying performance. Were those runs amassed against a weak attack on a perfect batting track – a 'road', as we call it? Were those wickets tail-end rabbits knocked over on a dodgy pitch? Stats are all very well but rarely do they tell the full story. Much better to ask: Did I prepare properly? Did I analyse opponents thoroughly? Did I follow my pre-match morning routine? Did I check the wicket? Did I take an appropriate guard for each bowler? When I got out, did I play the shot I intended correctly, and were my feet in position? All these things are questions of process. If any part of the process went wrong then learn from that and correct it. But don't judge yourself purely on the outcome. You might just have copped a good ball.

How to Read Cricket

Having made it to Z, here's a final thought: if players were judged solely on outcomes, then some of cricket's greatest players would never have emerged. Good coaches know this. They won't worry about a few poor performances, provided they can see underlying talent, dedication and a good attitude. That's so important for batters stepping up to international cricket because they need time to adjust and the assurance that they'll be given that time. Take Sri Lanka's Marvan Atapattu. His scores in the first six innings of his Test match career were 0, 0, 1, 0, 0, 0. Yet, over 17 years in the 1990s and 2000s, he would go on to prove himself among the most technically correct batters in the world, scoring 5,502 Test runs, including 16 centuries and six double centuries, plus a further 8,529 in ODIs. Atapattu eventually succeeded because process conquered outcomes. And because his coaches could read the way he played cricket.

Glossary

Agricultural shot A wild slog by a lower-order batter, usually in the direction of deep, wide mid-on. That fielding position is more popularly known as cow corner and so an agricultural shot is also dubbed a 'cow shot'. Personally, I call it the Chiropractor on the basis that it's guaranteed to put your back out.

Ashes, The Name for any Test match series between England and Australia. Its etymology is too long for a glossary but it comes down to a nineteenth-century English defeat, the burning of bails and a small wooden urn.

Average A bowler's average is the number of runs conceded divided by the number of wickets taken. A batter's average is the number of runs scored divided by the number of dismissals.

Bails The two 4.3-in. circular pieces of wood that sit on top of the stumps and that, in most circumstances, must be knocked off to get the batter out. Bail parts include the 'barrel' and the 'spigot'.

Bouncer A short-pitched ball, usually from a fast bowler, which rises up at the batter's head. Slow bouncers are sometimes used as a variation tactic in limited-overs cricket.

Bye A run taken from a delivery that touches neither batter nor bat. A leg bye is awarded if the ball strikes any part of the batter before the run is taken (unless the batter is out lbw).

Barnes Wallis Any ball that bounces several times before reaching the batter. Takes its name from the inventor of the wartime bouncing bomb, Sir Barnes Wallis. Balls bouncing more than once before reaching the popping crease are no-balls.

Cafeteria bowling Bowling that looks so easy to hit that the batter can help herself to runs. Also known as buffet bowling.

Cut A shot played square of, or behind, the wicket on the off side.

Declaration The action of a captain who voluntarily ends a Test innings – even though she still has players waiting to bat. She'll believe her team has enough runs to win but needs enough time to bowl out the opposition.

Dot ball A ball from which no run is scored. Takes its name from the dot in the scorebook to indicate this.

Drive A straight shot played back towards the bowler, usually in an arc between mid-off and mid-on.

Glossary

Eddie's extras Reference to the column in the scorebook that denotes wides, no-balls, byes and leg byes. Eddie regularly emerges as top-scorer in village games, while Pakistan holds the record for highest number of extras in Tests (76 against India at Bengaluru in 2007).

Five-fer Reference to a bowler taking five wickets in an innings.

Follow-on The tactical decision of a Test team batting first, requiring opponents to play their second innings immediately after their first. It can be enforced if the team batting second fails to get within 200 of their first-innings target. Handy, because the team enforcing the follow-on then knows how many runs, if any, they need to win.

Flashing hard Describes a batter's hefty swing outside off stump that may, or may not, make contact. I'm a big advocate. I was all for flashing hard because if the ball takes an edge it is likely to go through high or quickly, making slip chances harder. If you just stand there prodding away, there's more chance of an edge lobbing up for a simple catch. This is particularly true when it's a dodgy pitch, the ball is swinging, you're still settling in and you haven't got your feet moving into position. There'll be a ball with your name on it, so flash hard.

Full toss A ball that reaches the batter without bouncing. In limited-overs matches this is the worst possible delivery if it is also above waist height. This incurs a free hit on the next ball, making the batter immune to bowled, lbw or catch dismissals.

Going upstairs Referral to the third umpire following a disputed dismissal or a failed appeal.

Googly (aka wrong 'un) A ball from a right-arm leg spinner that turns like an off-break, ideally with no discernible difference in the bowler's action.

Grubscuttler A ball that barely bounces and instead shoots along the ground, theoretically massacring any unfortunate grubs pootering around the wicket. It usually happens on a wearing pitch – it can't be contrived – and it feels so unfair. The number of times I stepped back, ready to pull a short ball, only to see it bounce, die and grubscuttle into my pads or wicket.

Hogging Where one batter farms the strike by pushing a single at the end of an over to ensure she's facing at the start of the next.

Hook An aerial leg-side shot played behind square, typically to a bouncer.

Infield circle In limited-overs cricket, a circular area extending 30 metres from each wicket into which a minimum number of fielders, depending on the stage of the game, must be placed. This makes it harder for the fielding side to defend boundaries and encourages big-hitting among batters.

Inside out A difficult, counterintuitive shot in which a batter creates the space to turn a leg-side ball into an off-side shot. Often involves hitting against the spin – risky for the unwary. Requires good footwork and fast hands.

Glossary

Jaffa Describes any top-class ball. For me, the perfect Test match jaffa is one that pitches, shapes away from the batter and hits the top of off stump. Jimmy Anderson bowls those for fun.

King pair Being out for a duck in both innings of a Test match. Batters lie awake at night thinking about it.

LBW Stands for 'leg before wicket'. A form of dismissal in which the ball (a) strikes the batters pads or body, not including the gloves, before it hits the bat and (b) would have gone on to hit the wickets. There are caveats. See O for Out.

Leg spin The art of spinning a ball so that it changes course on landing. For example, leg spin from a right-handed bowler would turn from left to right as it is faced by a right-handed batter. For left-handers the definition changes accordingly.

Long hop A common sight on the village green, this is a slow ball pitched so short that it balloons tamely into the air – usually for prompt dispatch to the boundary.

Loosener Almost the Law in village cricket, this describes the first ball of a new bowler's spell. Often a ballooning full toss or an embarrassing wide, it is rare in the professional game and consequently never forgotten when it does happen. The most famous loosener of recent years was Steve Harmison's first delivery in the first Ashes Test of the 2006–7 series. It was so wide it was taken at second slip.

Maiden An over that concedes no runs or extras. In my nine-year international career, I only ever managed to bowl two. When I get stick for that, I insist my job was to take wickets, not save runs. It's unclear why we call it a maiden. One theory is that, historically, maiden meant 'unmarried' or 'untouched', so an over conceding no runs was a 'virgin' over.

Nightwatch A low-order Test batter sent in when a wicket falls to see out the final few overs over the day. The aim is to avoid exposing a top-order batter to a tricky period of play. Personally, I never see the point. Put in the player who best knows how to bat.

Nurdle Any non-boundary shot pushed into a gap. My former England team-mate Beth Morgan was an arch-nurdler. It was so frustrating for the fielding side, who would set their field carefully only to see her nudge the ball into space and rotate the strike.

Off (or leg) cutter Produced by fast- or medium-pace bowlers, a cutter is subtly different from a seaming ball. It relies partly on spin for movement rather than landing the seam in precisely the right position. For example, an off-cutter from a right-handed bowler turns from right to left as the right-handed batter faces it. For left-handers the definition changes accordingly.

Off for light Description of a break in play due to gathering gloom. Sympathy often lies with the batter in such circumstances because having a small, hard ball hurled towards you from 20 yards, at anything up to 100 mph, is daunting at the best of times. But at least the batter knows which direction it's coming from; fielders will often have no idea whether the ball is heading their way. This is true both in village cricket, where bracken is the backdrop, or the professional game where the ball is coming out of the crowd. Either way, it can be devilishly hard to spot.

Off spin The art of spinning a ball so that it changes course on landing. For example, off spin from a right-handed bowler would turn from right to left as it is faced by a right-handed batter. For left-handers and leg spinners the definition changes accordingly.

Outfield circle The fielding area outside the infield circle (see above).

Over A minimum of six balls – more if there are no-balls and wides – after which the bowling end switches and the non-striking batter is placed on strike. In addition, a right-handed bowler is said to be bowling 'over' the wicket if she delivers the ball with the wicket to her right. A right-hander is bowling 'around' the wicket if she delivers the ball with the wicket to her left. For left-handed bowlers . . . oh, you work it out.

Powerplay In limited-overs cricket, the Powerplay comprises pre-set periods of the match during which fielders are restricted to an infield circle, encouraging batters to hit past them to score boundaries. See P for Powerplay.

Plumb A clear lbw dismissal where the ball hits the batter's pads before hitting her bat. If that point of contact is below the knee roll of the pad, and you're bang in front of the stumps, everyone knows you're plumb, including you.

Pull A shot square of, or just behind, the wicket on the leg side.

Quick single A risky single run.

Rabbit (aka bunny) Derogatory term for a lower-order player who has dubious batting ability and is not expected to last long at the crease. It may stem from the phrase 'Like a rabbit caught in headlights'.

Red-ball game Refers to Test matches in international and county cricket. A red ball is also used in most club and village matches.

Rib-tickler A fast ball that rises unexpectedly, cannoning into the batter's chest. I experienced a few when practising to face Australia's quicks. The coaches at Loughborough thought it would be a neat idea to have us face England Under-17 male bowlers, one of whom was undeniably quick. Young guys don't want to be embarrassed by a girl so they send down fast bouncers straight away. One such delivery cannoned into the side of my ribs and I had to pretend it didn't hurt. It hurt like hell and turned into a monster bruise.

Skier The flight of a ball that sails high after being struck. It can often provide a catching chance in the outfield.

Shoulder arms The action of a batter who has decided a ball is too risky to play and so lifts her bat away high above her head. Looks good when it works but tragic when it is misjudged and stumps clatter.

Slog Once a scathing description of any aggressive, ugly swing by a batter, the term has in recent years been partially

Glossary

rehabilitated as an accepted limited-overs shot – particularly in a tense run-chase.

Square It can describe the playing area on which wickets are prepared but also defines the line of certain shots. Hitting 'square' would describe a ball struck at roughly 90 or 270 degrees to the on-strike batter. For example, hitting 'behind square' would describe a ball dispatched to the long leg fielding position (see diagram at the front of this book).

Striker The batter who is 'on strike' – in other words, preparing to receive the ball. Her partner at the other end is the non-striker.

Stumps The three circular 'sticks' at either end of the pitch that batters must defend and the fielding side try to strike. There is an off, middle and leg stump, although their identity changes depending on whether a left or right-handed batter is at the crease. For example, a right-handed batter's off stump will be the one furthest to the left as the bowler looks down the pitch. For a left-handed batter, though, this would become the leg stump.

Super Over Used in the event of a tie in limited-overs cricket. Each team chooses three batters as their line-up for a single over. If two get out, the over immediately ends. If both teams end with the same number of runs, a second Super Over may ensue, depending on tournament rules.

Teapot The typical posture of a bowler who has watched yet another catching chance downed by the slips. One hand will be on the hip, the other out wide, palm uppermost, in a gesture of incredulity.

Twelfth man/woman The first substitute who comes on to replace an injured player. They also get dogsbody tasks such as taking replacement kit out to batters.

Uppish An aerial batting shot offering a potential outfield catch. It can be legitimate if you're trying to clear the inner circle of fielders but the danger lies in playing a slower ball too early and spooning it into waiting hands.

Village A scathing noun used for any bumbling or incompetent player. As in 'that's so village'. Often muttered by club cricketers who think they're better than they are.

Wicket Confusingly, this can refer to the playing surface ('it's a decent wicket'), the stumps at either end ('that nearly hit the wicket') or something the batter possesses ('she surrendered her wicket').

Wobble seam A seam bowler's unconventional grip that is supposed to make the ball act unpredictably on bounce. When it does, it's pure luck.

White-ball game Refers to T20 (20 overs a side) and ODI (50 overs a side) games as both formats use a white instead of a red ball.

xR and xW Data metrics representing 'expected runs' and 'expected wickets'. Techies use them during games to indicate likely outcomes or afterwards to show how and why

Glossary

things went pear-shaped. Take a deep breath before delving further.

Yorker A ball that pitches under or just beyond the bat. Notoriously difficult to bowl and even more difficult to play. In women's cricket, West Indies' Deandra Dottin is brilliant at them. In the modern men's game there have been few better exponents than Sri Lanka's Lasith Malinga and the Pakistan pair of Waqar Younis and Wasim Akram.

Zip Description of a ball that 'kisses' the pitch and bounces up quicker than expected.